On the Cover: **Medicine Crow (Sacred Raven)** He led a dozen successful raids and counted coup by stealing horses and became chief of the Mountain Crow tribe at the young age of 20. Chief Medicine Crow was successful on the battlefield. The Chief conquered his enemies and took many scalps and became a famous chief, medicine man and visionary of the Crow. On the back cover- **"The Vanishing American,"** A Crow war-chief rides into the sunset.

Note: The word squaw is not a guttural term. Squaw in the Algonquian language family in the Narragansett Indian tongue simply meant an Indian woman or wife. The word, squaw was later adapted into the English language. Some Native American women may think squaw to be demeaning, but it is not. I like to use it at times, with no ill intent, because it is a colorful word used back in the past for an Indian woman and is politically correct.

1

Dedication Page
This work is dedicated to
my wife & family

THE MEDICINE CROW INDIANS

THE TRIBE THAT BEFRIENDED THE WHITE MAN

ROBERT D. BOLEN

Yellowstone's Grand Canyon
(Courtesy of Ned Eddins)

PHOTOGRAPHS

Edward S. Curtis, the master photographer of the 19th century has captured iconic images of hundreds of American Indians like no one else. His mission was to document the Indians in time. The ceremonies, dress, and culture come to life in print. With the camera, Curtis has caught a glimpse in time of days gone by on photogravure with narrative. Curtis has portrayed the lifestyle of a forgotten era. He has taken the pictures of Indian chiefs, warriors, braves, women, elderly men and women, princesses, papooses in their native habit. Curtis captured a segment of culture that will never return to America.

Over 80 American Indian tribes were his subjects from the Plateau region to the American Southwest filling volumes. His unparalleled photos of the American Native are masterpieces. Curtis' glass plate negatives now nearly two centuries old are truly fascinating. Edward S. Curtis has captured on film the greatest collection of American Indians ever photographed and archived.

I would like to especially thank Theresa Harbaugh of Denver, Colorado and Azusa Publishing Company, L.L.C. com. for allowing me to borrow these wonderful photos for my books.

MAPS AND ILLUSTRATIONS

CONTENTS
CHAPTERS

Chief Plenty Coups in buffalo skin coat
(Courtesy of Nez Perce.com)

ACKNOWLEDGEMENTS

My deepest thanks go out to Teresa, owner of Azusa Publishing, L.L.C., in Denver, Colorado for all of the wonderful iconic Indian post cards, she has graciously allowed me to use in this text. The 1800's Curtis photos are superb and really make the book in my estimation. Her website address and ad for authentic Indian postcards is in the back of the book. I highly recommend you view her fine web site and peruse the authentic pix and make an order.

I would like to thank the Smithsonian Institute for the old picture of Washakie's village.

I offer kudos, to Bonnie Fitzpatrick of the Designer for her formatting and graphic design. Bonnie does a great job!

My thanks go out to Len Sodenkamp for his artist's abilities in the excellent drawing and interpretation of the "Buffalo Hunter on Horseback."

I would like to thank Michael Gray for his bison photo in Yellowstone and Ned Eddins for his photos of interest in Wyoming.

Last, but not least, my sincerest thanks to Lightning Source (Ingram Publishing Company) for their fine job of printing this publication.

"Wopila tanka," many thanks to all, in the Siouan tongue of the Crow Indians!

FOREWORD

The Crow Indians can make the claim that they were a Plains Indian tribe, who as a majority never warred against America, but one renegade tribe did make war with the U. S. Army.

The majority of the Crow were peaceable and friendly to the white-man from the beginning. Their chiefs were given coveted peace medals awarded to peaceable American Indian chiefs by U.S. Presidents.

The Crow tribe was one of the few Plains Indians to remain neutral and friendly to the Euro-American settlers and U.S. Army for over 50 years and never once warred against the United States until 1887.

One rebel chief led his band in the Crow War and was the one exception. A brief incursion was staged with Chief Sword Bearer and The U.S. Army called the Crow Indian War, but that was the exception. The Crow Indians who attacked the Johnson cabin were in the minority.

When the Sioux declared war on the United States, hundreds of Crow Indian warriors volunteered as U.S. Army scouts to fight their old enemy, the Sioux and served in many campaigns.

The Crow Indians were loyal guides and scouts for the Army, who found the enemy's trail and spied on them. The Crow Indian tribe provided the very best Indian scouts for the U.S. Army. The Army outfitted them with guns and ammo, horses and goods.

Our thanks go out to the hundreds of Crow Indians that have volunteered, fought, and died in the military to defend our country.

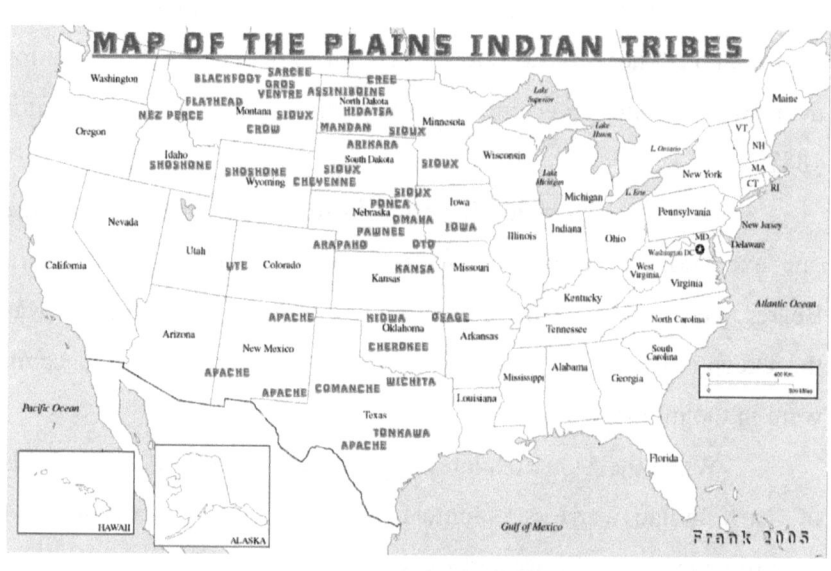

Map Courtesy of frank'srealm.com

CHAPTER ONE
CROW ORIGINS

Archeologists believe that natives came across the natural land bridge of the Bering Straits from Siberia shortly after the Ice Age. Aboriginal ancestors of the Hidatsa Indians probably emerged onto the continent the same way to follow migrating herds of bison across Alaska, Canada into the Great Lakes region. Information gathered from the Archeological record, oral tradition and ancient narratives tells us the Hidatsa became a hunter/farmer society, circa 1400 A.D. Hidatsa farmers dwelled for centuries in earthen lodges.

Chief Raven Face ruled in 1400 A.D. The Crow tribe is historically associated with the Hidatsa (Minnataree) and according to Indian legend, the Hidatsa tribe, the ancestral tribe of the Crow Indians, dwelled in the land of forests and lakes in the Upper Great Lakes region of Canada and northern America centuries ago.

According to legend, in 1450 A.D., one band split off from the Hidatsa tribe and migrated westward from the Great Lakes across the Mississippi River along the Middle Missouri, near communities of Arikara and Mandan Indians, who were agrarian farmers in present day North Dakota. The Hidatsa Indians planted beans, corn, squash and tobacco. They hunted game, made pottery and crafted baskets, since they were sedentary Indians.

Hidatsa villages were permanent subterranean earthen lodges halfway underground and well insulated. The earth shelters were built around a central plaza, surrounded by a log barrier nearly 12 feet in height by 14 feet in diameter, which deterred enemy invasions.

Buffalo in the Teton Range
(Photograph Courtesy of Ned Eddins)

About 1450, two Hidatsas, No Intestines and Red Scout trekked to Devil's Lake, North Dakota and fasted. Red Scout settled on the Missouri, learned to grow crops from the Mandan and envisioned sacred tobacco. Paints-His-Shirt-Red was the chief in the early 1500's. The Hidatsa dwelled on the Missouri, circa, 1550 A.D. Mid 1500's, Chief Red Fish's his band controlled the obsidian mines in Yellowstone. Running Coyote, in the late 1500's had a vision of great medicine and developed the buffalo jump for procuring meat.

The Crow Indian tribe is named for the American crow, a large songbird with black plumage that makes a harsh call. The flock feeds together, as a sentinel keeps watch. Noisy heckling crows give shrill calls, wings flapping. Crows roost together in hoards in the winter time and rob eggs. A larger crow species is called the raven.

According to legend we know the Crow Indians split from the Hidatsa tribe in 1600 A.D. as an offshoot band that called themselves the Aparsokee, (children of the big beaked bird). Other tribes referred to them as the Crow. Neighbors flapped their arms imitating bird wings, describing the Crow in the American Indian sign language.

The Crow divided into two bands and were far ranging. One group formed the Mountain Crow and lodged in the Bighorn Mountains of present day southern Montana and northern Wyoming. The other formed the River Crow that dwelled along the Yellowstone.

Another split from the Hidatsa occurred, circa 1600 A.D., as women argued on the Missouri over dividing a drowned bison. Bad Heart Bear's wife complained of not receiving enough tripe, which caused the split; his band joined the River Crow.

15

The Hidatsa and Crow spoke the Siouan dialect. Though they spoke the common language of the Sioux Indians, the Crow and Sioux were bitter enemies fighting over territory and their hunting grounds. Other Crow enemies were the Blackfeet and Shoshoni. In 1640 A.D., Jesuit priests contacted Siouan speakers.

The Dakota Indians were driven out of the Great Lakes region to the Upper Mississippi region by enemy Chippewa Indians using horses and firearms bartered from the English.

The earliest written record of the Crow was by James Knight of the Hudson's Bay Company trading post at the York Factory on the Hudson's Bay in Canada in 1716 A.D. He wrote that he was visited by "Mountain Indians," who had Crow Indian slaves.

Leadership was similar role among the plains tribes. A band had a chief if in a village. A warrior completed four difficult war deeds to become chief.

War chiefs earned their rank on the field of battle and chose warriors as sub-chiefs under them. A band was a group of Plains Indians that wandered behind the herds and had camp chiefs. A band leader was chosen to direct an activity.

A man paid "bride price" for a wife, married her younger sisters as younger wives. Polygamy is to have more than one spouse. A woman could marry her husband's younger brothers. A widow could marry her deceased husband's younger brothers.

There are six distinct kin naming systems in the world. Three are the American Indian: the Crow, Omaha, and Iroquois. The Omaha kin system is patrilineal descent traced through the father's line.

The Crow clan system practiced matrilineal lineage and polygamy. Matrilineal is tracing descent though the mother's line as found in the Crow line of descent.

Family was the basic unit. Matrilocal is the term used when the residence was with the wife's mother's family. The brave had to marry a young woman from another clan to avoid incest in the family.

In Crow descent, children were born into the mother's group and took her clan name. The mother's blood relatives were all related and it was taboo for a man to belong to the same clan as his children; one exception was if the mother married a member of her own clan.

In the matrilineal Crow system relatives were grouped together on the basis of descent and gender. Siblings and parallel cousins of the same gender are given the same term of reference. A parallel cousin is a cousin who is the child of one's mother's sister or one's father's brother. Mother and sister have the same kin name.

In matrilineage, only parallel cousins are relatives; in ego's father's matrilineage, his relatives were grouped across generations reflecting the comparative unimportance of the father's side of the family that strongly follows the matrilineal principle of descent.

Some cousins are regarded as brother and sisters, aunts as mothers and uncles as fathers. Parallel cousins are ego's father's brother's children, and mother's, sister's children. The cross cousins are ego's father's sister's children and mother's brother's children.

The family was and is the emphasis of the Crow people. The family came first and was of the most importance. After that, clan and tribe followed. Elders of the tribe are and were respected then and now.

American Indians of the Great Plains
Courtesy of AOL

18

CHAPTER TWO

MOUNTAIN CROW

From oral tradition and the archeological record we learned the Crow Indians separated from the Hidatsa tribe on the Missouri and a number became the Mountain Crow Indians in the 17th century, moving into the Bighorn Valley Mountain range of the Rockies.

The Mountain Crow inhabited the Rocky Mountains, where the Bighorn, Powder, Rosebud, Tongue and Wind River flow into the Yellowstone to the Laramie River as far as the Platte River and lodged northwest of the Platte to the source of the Musselshell.

They were a politically distinct division of the Crow tribe that ranged from the mouth of the Bighorn Canyon, south to the Bighorn Basin into the Wind River and Pryor Mountains in Bighorn Mountain country, in southern Montana and northern Wyoming.

The Kiowa moved from western Montana into Yellowstone and the Black Hills, circa, 1700 A.D. as close allies of the Crow Indians, but the Sioux drove the Kiowa from the Black Hills to the Arkansas River.

From legend we know that a band of Crow Indians camped at the conjunction of the Bighorn and Little Bighorn Rivers and entertained French-Canadian trappers passing through Crow country in 1743.

There the Kiowa's militant Chief Dogs fought the Comanche Indian tribe until 1790, when they had reached an agreement and signed a peace treaty. The Comanche, Kiowa and Kiowa-Apache formed an Alliance. They bonded intermarried, hunted and warred together.

The Kiowa Indians are noted for originating sign language and were prolific sign talkers on the Plains, along with the Teton Dakota (Sioux). The American Indian sign language is still used today, primarily at ceremonies, festivals and intertribal powwows.

Montana Territory was Blackfeet Indian country and also home to the Mountain Crow. The Blackfeet lodged not far from the Crow Indians in buffalo country and were possessive of their lands.

It was recorded that Mountain Indians, who owned Crow slaves, had visited the Hudson Bay Company trading post at York's factory in Canada. Another early reference was by fur trader Jean Baptiste Trudeau who noted that a war party of "Ricaras" (Arikara Indians) arrived on June 5, 1795 with a Mountain Crow Indian scalp.

The Crow male did not marry until he reached 25 or had taken his first coup. Young Crows were instructed to count coup by touching the enemy. He had to touch the enemy with his hand, bow or quirt.

The first raid to take enemy horses counted as coup and going on a war party into battle for scalps was important in becoming a man; warriors described feats and sang songs of war. Joining a military society was significant. Plains Indians had a militant culture.

A simple coup stick was a green willow staff with a few eagle feathers. A full coup stick was a long green willow limb soaked in water and bent at the end and tied in a hook. The finished product was a sacred medicine coup stick decorated with feathers, otter fur, and paint used to count coup by touching the enemy.

The Indians' word for scout and wolf were nearly synonymous. The Crow braves applied mud to their bodies for

20

"Shot-in-the-Hand"
Mountain Crow Warrior
(Photograph Courtesy of Azusa Publishing, LLC)

camouflage and added mud ears to resemble the grey wolf. They prepared for the raid as Crow-Wolves, the name of their society.

Crow warriors (Wolves) that belonged to the Wolf Society wore the wolf head and skin and over their head and shoulders on night raids. The power of the wolf and the warrior's strength formed a bond in warfare. The wolf fur touching the skin transferred power.

The Crow were members of their own militant societies. The Wolves were a militant society of the Crow Indians. Hundreds of members of the Crow Indian Wolf society became U.S. Army Scouts in 1876 and proved to be excellent guides, soldiers and scouts.

The atlatl was a throwing apparatus used in hunting large game as early as 13,000 B.P. The spear had an 8 inch fore-shaft with a spear head and hollow reed or wooden shaft and was thrown by way of a strap on a wooden thruster with finger-loops and a hook for the spear at elbows' length for 100 yards, to bring down a mammoth or bison-bison. A weight was added for momentum.

Sometime in the past came the bow and arrow. They crafted fine bows from sheep horn and made bows and arrows of birch, oak, mountain mahogany, mountain yew and other suitable hardwoods. A good bow may have been wrapped with rattlesnake skin. Bow strings were animal gut. Eagle or hawk feathers were used to fletch an arrow.

The Crow Indians crafted fine bows and arrows which were admired by other tribes. A shaft was heated, straightened, smoothed and polished for an arrow. Marking arrow feathers was custom. Indians flint knapped (chipped) arrow heads from chert and inserted them into a slit in the end of the shaft, glued with pitch and wrapped with sinew.

Crow Indian & Medicine Coup Stick
(Photograph Courtesy of Azusa Publishing, LLC)

The war shield often meant the difference between life and death in battle and saved the warrior from an arrow, bullet or spear. To make a war shield a warrior cut a thick circular piece of buffalo hide from the shoulders region, about four feet in diameter and had a squaw remove the hair from the hide.

Dirt was spread over a pit fire with rocks in it. The skin was then laid over the dirt. The medicine shield was painted with sacred symbols of the warrior's totem, adorned with eagle feathers, ermine skins and eagle talons.

The Crow purchased dances from other tribes for their societies. Societies normally evolved from a dream and became established. Feasts songs and dances were societal. The music was played on drums, flutes, mariachis, rattles and eagle-bone whistles. The dancers sang as they danced while a chorus of singers chanted.

There were dances for men only through the societies and some strictly for women. The Crow learned the Bear Dance from the Hidatsa, but refused to dance it exactly the same. The Bear Dance Song was sung in accompaniment. Crow Dances were the Buffalo Dance, Grass Dance, Horse Dance, Scalp Dance, Victory Dance and the War Dance. The Crow did the Medicine Pipe Ritual Dance.

The Crow tribe sang favorite songs to attract the buffalo to their camp, when game was scarce. Crow Indians like the Mandan and Sioux did the Buffalo Dance to call the buffalo to come to them.

The Crow warriors wore fringed deerskin war shirts, leggings and sometimes moccasins and the squaws wore fringed deerskin dresses, leggings and moccasins. They adorned their clothing with bead-work, quill-work and blue, green, red and yellow paint.

24

Yellowstone Bison
(Courtesy of Mike Gray @ Nampa.net)

A ring of feathers 8 to 10 inches across, that fanned out in a circle was called a "crow" and was worn on the back of the waist and a slightly smaller crow was worn on the back of the head in the hair.

In 1843, Emperor Maximilian I of Mexico estimated the Crow dwelled in 400 lodges and possessed 9,000-10,000 horses. He described them as a people proud of their features and long hair.

Maximilian depicted the Mountain Crow dress and liked their war shirts and dresses made of bighorn sheep leather and embroidered buffalo robes adorned with colorful dyed porcupine quills. He praised the Crow squaws for their amount of hard work.

Maximilian marveled at the beautiful workmanship on the warrior's bow and arrows and was quite impressed with how they expertly made long bows of inlaid elk horn and bighorn sheep horn, covered with rattlesnake skins and commented on their excellent riding and warring skills He remarked about their very unusual platform burials. The platform burials and tree burials were quite different.

Young Crow braves orchestrated simulated battles against each other. They chose up sides and fought mock battles and enacted their going to war, which helped prepare the braves for actual combat with the enemy.

The Crow built communal sweat lodges used by the men to socialize. They built a lodge and utilized stones to wall up a running hot springs of natural spring water of minerals healthy for natural body cleansing. After the sweat bath, they took a cold plunge.

Red Bear was a Mountain Crow chieftain in the 1840's and well remembered among the Crow people.

"Medicine Crow," (Sacred Raven), a Mountain Crow (Apsarokee) Indian, was the son of the great chief, "Joined Together" and his wife, "One-Buffalo-Calf" on the Musselshell River in 1848.

Medicine Crow was taught to craft a bow and arrows and shoot targets and soon began to hunt rabbits, squirrels and game birds. He competed with the other young braves in foot races and wrestling with them in the grass. Medicine Crow swam in their swimming hole.

He was given a pony and learned to ride at a young age; he raced his pony and could ride to the side to dodge arrows or shoot under his horse's head and pull a comrade up behind him.

At twelve years old, Medicine Crow reached the age of puberty and went into seclusion in the tribal fasting grounds to attain his vision quest. He fasted and prayed for four days until he saw his vision of his visionary helper (Spirit guide).

Medicine Crow was strong and grew in stature. He had a vision as a young brave that if he dealt fairly with the white man things would turn out for his people's good. Medicine Crow listened to tales as a youth and heard stories of warrior's deeds.

He first entered into combat at fifteen and became a great chief of the Kicked-in-Their-Bellies band, circa 1870, at twenty two years of age.

He was a visionary medicine man chief and led a dozen successful raids, killed the enemy, stole horses and took scalps and had two horses shot out from under him.

Medicine Crow led three braves on a raid for horses to present day Cody, Wyoming capturing four Shoshoni ponies, which were given to relatives, as was custom. He received his first honor.

The Sioux fought the Crow at present day, Hardin, Montana. Two Crows rode by and knocked a warrior off his horse, striking the first and second coups. Medicine Crow wrestled with the warrior and wrested his rifle from him, gaining his second war honor.

Chief Medicine Crow led a war party against a Sioux camp which is now Forsyth, Montana, and sent warriors to steal horses. They failed; he rode in and cut the halter rope of a fine pony tied to a tipi door, counted coup and stole two buffalo-war horses and a mule.

A Nez Perce warrior used sign language asking Crows to kill him. Medicine Crow and a comrade gave out boisterous war whoops and rode toward him, but the warrior shot both of their horses.

Medicine Crow ran toward him in a zigzag motion. The brave reloaded, fired and hit him under the arm; he dropped his powder horn, dove onto him and wrested his rifle away, and counted coup.

In 1874, a Crow war party attacked the Sioux, killing seven braves on Tulloch Creek east of the Crow Agency. The Sioux were holed up in a wash firing on them killing several, when Medicine Crow dodged arrows and bullets and sprinted toward them. Medicine Crow dove into the trench. The warriors fled. He received war honors for the assault and for capturing the enemy's weapon.

Crows camped on Pryor Creek, when Arapahoe braves were sighted. They rode hard toward the ravine with Medicine Crow hot on their trail. His fast horse caught up to them, but was shot out from under him; as he fell, he wrestled with the Arapahoes pulling them off their ponies with him. He counted coup, taking a brave's weapon and as he rode back, Medicine Crow sang the "song of war."

"Wolf" Mountain Crow Medicine Man
(Photograph Courtesy of Azusa Publishing, LLC)

The Crow and Sioux warred on Pass Creek south of present day, Wyola, Montana. One warrior outfought the Crows, his medicine, strong. The Sioux warrior seemed to evade both arrows and bullets.

Medicine Crow called on his protector, the eagle (striped tail). He took careful aim with his muzzle-loader and fired, the Sioux fell from his horse. Medicine Crow rushed in and struck his first coup and took his weapon. He counted the second coup and took his scalp.

Medicine Crow had a great vision of the buffalo herds dwindling away and the coming of the white man. It is quite obvious that the prophecy came true.

The Chief had a vision of Crow country covered with large herds of white man's cattle (horse buffalo). He had another vision of his home (a white man's house) atop a hill that overlooked the place where Grass Lodge Creek flows into the Little Bighorn River where he built his home in 1905.

Medicine Crow became a reservation chief and later developed skills as an artist. The chief visited Washington D.C. to see the great white father and sketched many animals in the Washington Zoo that are in existence, today!

Medicine Crow died in July of 1920 and was buried on a hill over the "Valley of Chieftains." The tribal elders spoke of his great deeds. His friend, Bird-Far-Away recorded his deeds on a 3 x 22 foot strip of cloth in hieroglyphics, owned by Joseph Medicine Crow.

Shoshoni warrior, "Coyote Appears" and his Crow Indian wife, "It-Might-Have-Happened," had a son, Medicine Bird.

30

"Medicine Bird" and "Otter Woman" had a son. His birth name was "Buffalo-Facing-the-Wind," born the same year as Medicine Crow.

When he was just a small boy, Buffalo-Facing-the-Wind's father gave him a toy cedar bow and four arrows. Later, Coyote Appears made a crude cottonwood bow and arrow and he was instructed in its use. His grandfather used a buffalo chip for a target. He could shoot and hit the chip three out of five times and then shot moving targets. At seven years old, he was given a genuine bow with iron tipped arrows his father had bartered from the trading post.

As a child, the boy was taught the lessons in life by his grandfather, Coyote Appears, who taught him to be alert, strong, and steadfast. He was fleet of foot and loved to race. One day, grandfather, a wise old sage, told him to strip down to his loin cloth and moccasins and said to catch a yellow butterfly.

The boy ran like a deer, as the butterfly flitted away and returned with the delicate creature cupped in his hands. Grandfather told the boy to ask it to give him grace and swiftness and then to release it.

A beaver was caught and its flat tail was used to strike the muscles in the body for conditioning and to teach them its power in the water. Buffalo-Facing-the-Wind learned wisdom from animals in nature, lessons learned from the butterfly and the beaver.

He became proficient with targets and hunted rabbits and squirrels with his friends. Soon he hunted game and put food on the dinner table as a hunter now and a young warrior. His grandfather had taught him, well. He was becoming a man. Braves dived into a lake in winter conditions, with chunks of ice floating in it to condition the body and taught to do a flip; if they failed, they were dunked.

Grandfather killed a huge brown bear, skinned and dressed it. He removed the heart and held it up. Buffalo-Facing-the-Wind was expected to eat some of the raw heart to gain its strength.

During puberty Crow braves experienced an ordeal to obtain their "medicine dream" (vision quest) and gain a name. He went into the mountains in seclusion for four days on his vision quest.

So Buffalo-Facing-the-Wind fasted and prayed until he saw his vision. He received his medicine (powers) and claimed the strength of the spirit of the Chickadee.

Buffalo–Facing-the-Wind was given a pony as a lad and learned to ride. He raced his pony with the other braves and learned to retrieve a cloth off the ground from the saddle, pull a comrade up behind him onto his horse and lay over to one side of his pony to dodge arrows and shoot under his pony's head to avoid arrows.

Also on the plains, counting coup was a mark of manhood by touching the enemy, stealing his weapon or horse. Counting coup was accomplished by running in or riding up and touching the enemy, whether alive or dead or capturing an enemy's weapon. A bow, lance or the brave's hand was used in "counting coup" to touch the enemy.

A brave deed merited an eagle feather and feathers were worn to designate bravery. A split feather indicated wounding an enemy. Killing an enemy was marked by a hole in the quill of a feather. Plenty Coups earned eagle feathers for many coups and received 80 honors. Plenty Coups was an admired chief. He was an honorable leader of his people.

Buffalo–Facing-the-Wind led a raiding party to steal horses on a moonlit night. A war party was formed and they rode to the enemy camp. Two braves acted as scouts.

A member of the Wolf Society held the horses, while others crawled beneath wolf skins and entered into the encampment. Buffalo-Facing-the-Wind cut the halter rope holding a horse, counting coup. He led it silently from camp and mounted the pony. Leading a successful war party counted as his first war deed. He had met the requirements to become chief.

The role of tribal chief was gained by heroism on the battlefield and cunning on the hunt. Plenty-Coups became a champion of the people who voted him principal Chief of the Mountain Crows in 1876; He was 25 years old. Plenty Coups fashioned a headdress of eagle feathers fitting for a chief. If a Crow chief successfully led a war party on a raid, he was entitled to wear ermine skins on his war shirt as a trophy. The act of touching an enemy counted as one coup.

Coyote Appears had a dream where he saw his grandson taking many coups with strong medicine and that someday Buffalo-Facing-the-Wind would become a great war-chief. Coyote Appears knew Aleek-chea-ahoosh, meaning Plenty Coups or Many Achievements was to be his grandson's name.

When Buffalo-Facing-the-Wind became a man, having acquired many coups, he changed his name to Plenty Coups, just as his grandfather Coyote Appears had foretold.

Medicine Crow and Plenty Coups were friends, as were Two Leggings and Bird-Far-Away. Their friendships were lasting. These Chiefs were revered in their tribe.

One day a Sioux war party approached. The Crow did not want a fight. There were women and children in camp and no time to escape with little choice but to stand and fight. The enemy was upon them. War whoops and rifle fire filled the air as Crow warriors on horses formed a circle of protection around the camp.

The Sioux warriors stayed out away from the perimeter, circling and firing in the dirt, short of the Crow warriors, as they used up their ammunition. Chief Iron Bull ordered them to hold their fire. The Sioux chiefs wore their fancy war bonnets. The action slowed and a Sioux chief gave a war cry and wheeled his horse out of the ranks. He spurred the pony toward the Crow then rode parallel to them, his war bonnet hung down to the ground flailing in the breeze.

The Sioux chief was within rifle range, two rifle cracks blazed; the horse and rider dropped. Little Fire and Gun Chief fired together and claimed coup, but the chief was on his feet running. Swan's Head spurred his horse and struck the chief with his quirt, but the Sioux turned and shot Swan's Head in the chest, severely wounding him and continued to run to safety. Chief Iron Ball ordered Plenty Coups and his band of 40 Crow warriors to avenge the deaths.

He-Is-Brave-Without-Being-Married took up the chase to avenge Swan's Head being shot. As he struck the warrior with his coup stick, the Sioux warrior fired and killed him.

A Sioux riding a white horse pulled the warrior up behind him. Plenty Coups fired, knocked them down and attempted to ride over the warrior, but the Sioux fired and killed his horse. At that moment, the mighty Sioux warrior and his comrade were up on their feet running away.

Chief Medicine Crow
(Photograph Courtesy of Azusa Publishing, LLC)

Chief Plenty Coups' uncle, Long Horse brought a horse for him. Plenty Coup took chase. Crazy Wolf was shot dead as he rode up to the fleeing Sioux. Plenty Coups feared that his friend would be scalped, but the Sioux took his rifle and kept running. He killed the warrior. The Crow and Nez Perce won the fight with the Sioux and drove them off. Many died; the Crow captured 200 horses.

The Crow Indians moved camp to the Elk River (Yellowstone) to avoid the Lakota. Swan's Head was barely alive. Plenty Coups' heart sang. Plenty Coups put him on his horse and led him to camp. They carried his litter into a lodge near the river. The medicine man tended his wounds, but he died four days later.

The Crow heard that roving Sioux attacked their River Crow allies, killed many and took horses, Plenty Coups and a Crow war party went on the war trail to avenge the wrongs. They swam the Yellowstone River and met the Red River traders, who were hunting buffalo at the time.

The traders were the Metis tribe, a French-Canadian Indian mix, who used wooden carts to haul their goods. The Indians did not bother them. The Metis seemed to fear the war party, but soon learned they were friendly. They gave the Crow Indians meat and tobacco for their pipes and informed them of a large Sioux camp to the east.

Crow scouts brought back word that the Sioux were readying for battle, but outnumbered them two to one. The Crow camp had 40 lodges of Nez Perce Indian visitors ready to fight. The next day the Crow located the Sioux village, stopped for a parley and smoked their pipes. The Wolves planned to lure the Sioux into an ambush.

"Plenty Coups, Chief of the Crows"
(Photograph Courtesy of Azusa Publishing, LLC)

The Crows were anxious to be able to stir up the Sioux and put their plan into action. The Wolves moved into position, when one Crow began to ride back and forth as a signal to retreat. A lone Sioux hunter rode directly toward Plenty Coups and his companions.

The Chief rode from the willows and fired hitting him in the calf and crippling his horse with a broken leg. Bull-That-Does-Not-Fall did not count coup on him. Horse and rider limped to the village.

Plenty Coups fired at some Sioux, who were swimming, but his horse shied at the rifle crack and he missed. His shooting poor all day, he fired up the whooping band of Sioux Indians, rode out behind Plenty Coups who raced towards the awaiting Crow, bullets striking all around him; they joined four other Crows and retreated to the rear.

Signal mirror flashes on a high bluff for them to come in that the Sioux numbers were too great. They hid, holding their horses, the only means of escape and heard the thunder of the hoofs as the war party rode past them.

The Sioux turned their ponies, retraced their tracks, split up and rode past the Crow again. Wolves stole horses.
Scalp Necklace took two scalps, but lost his in the Wolf Mountains.

Plenty Coups served as Chief Scout for General Crook in 1876. He held many feasts. Plenty Coups was called, "the chief of all chiefs." The chief fought to keep their land and kept their reservation on Crow lands. He helped them transition to the reserve.

Chief Plenty Coups was a great reservation chief and was the principal chief of the Crow Nation. The wise and honorable Chief Plenty Coups adhered to the traditions of the tribe and was loyal to the clan.

His life was honored at the dedication of the Tomb of the Unknown Soldier. Chief Plenty Coups was honored as the greatest tribal chieftain for his leader-ship. A famous quote of Chief, Plenty Coups was *"The ground on which we stand is sacred ground. It is the blood of our ancestors."*

Josiah Thomas Yellowtail was born in July of 1855, the son of pre-reservation Crow Indians, Rises Upward and Stays-by-the-Water. Yellowtail was the youngest son of Elizabeth Frazee Chienne and Yellowtail, the grandson of Chief Medicine Crow.

Tom Yellowtail's great grandfather, Pierre Chienne was the son of French immigrants a fur trader, mountain man, squaw-man, and interpreter for the Crow. Chienne represented the Crow at the 1868 Treaty of Laramie interpreting for Crow chief, "Blackfoot."

Tom's wife's name was Susie. They enrolled their children in the new Baptist Church day school; the Catholic Church in Lodge Grass excommunicated Yellowtail, so he joined the Baptist Church.

Yellowtail was a good Crow chief, holy man and medicine man, who danced the traditional Sun Dance. He fasted in the Sun Dance lodge and prayed with an eagle feather wand to heal the sick.

Yellowtail carried a carved effigy and attributed his success to it. He honored the traditions of the clan and earned five names, his favorite was "Medicine Rock Chief," given him by Chief Medicine Crow. At Fort Washakie, Wyoming, a famous Shoshoni medicine chief gave Yellowtail his eagle feather wand and made him a Sun Dance medicine man, last chief of the entire Crow Indian Nation.

The famous chiefs of the Crow Nation were war chiefs and led their bands to fight enemy tribes. They headed up raids to steal enemy horses. The Crow killed and scalped their enemies. They were fierce warriors and fought the strongest tribes and were a proud breed and lived by their traditions.

When the white man came, the Crow were friendly and peaceable toward them. The mighty chiefs traveled far to meet with the "Great White Father" in Washington D.C. Medicine Crow, Plenty Coups and Yellowtail were a few of these great chiefs. They stand out in history as heroes of the old west.

These chiefs were recipients of the special peace medals awarded to American Indian tribes that remained peaceable to the United States of America by the President of the United States for their excellence and cooperation.

Chiefs Medicine Crow and Plenty Coups were war chiefs and led the Mountain Crow "Wolves" and other bands of Crow to fight and heed the call of duty. When it came to the white man, the chiefs were their allies. They helped transition their people onto reservations and st a fine example for them.

These chiefs fall into the category of genuine "peace chiefs." They were of the finest character. When it came time to serve in the Indian Wars, the Crow Indian tribe was ready to fight the Sioux, their mortal enemies. The Crow not only fought in the past, but went on to serve in the World Wars. They volunteered, fought bravely and died heroically for their tribe and Americans everywhere.

The Crow people are of the finest character and integrity. It is easy to say that the Crow Indians have always been the friend of the people of the United States and that they always will be their allies.

CHAPTER THREE

THE RIVER CROW

After the split from the Hidatsa Indians, the Crow had learned to cultivate corn from the Mandan Indians along the Missouri River. Some farmed and others hunted. The River Crow moved west along the Yellowstone and settled into the Yellowstone River Basin on the Milk, Missouri and Yellowstone Rivers in Montana.

The River Crow also dwelled in the Judith and Musselshell River Valleys and slowly replaced agriculture by hunting buffalo, deer, elk and gathering berries, fleshy leaves, nuts, roots, seeds.

The River Crow continued trade with agrarian tribes to the east and maintained trade on the Missouri between the ancient Middle Missouri villages and the Shoshoni and Nez Perce of the Plateau. Mountain Crows traded west and the River Crow east.

The River Crow were now a separate autonomous group of the Crow tribe, but were homogeneous with the Mountain Crow. The Crow were fierce warriors with a strong socio-political structure. In the late 1700's the River Crow acquired the horse and moved onto the Plains, well after the Mountain Crow.

It was President Thomas Jefferson's belief in "Manifest Destiny" that it was inevitable for the United States to expand to the Pacific Coast. He commissioned Lewis and Clark to make the trek.

In 1804, Lewis and Clark dwelled at Fort Mandan. They met Charbonneau, a French Canadian trapper and his wife. Sacajawea. During the winter of 1805, Sacajawea had a son, they named, Jean Baptiste.

Crow Populations

1804	350 Lodges
1829	450 Lodges
1834	450 Lodges
1843	400 Lodges
1862	460 Lodges
1890	450 Lodges

Sacajawea was invaluable to Clark and led them to the Pacific. Early in 1805, Lewis and Clark met the Crow and Hidatsa Indians on the Missouri River. Clark called the Mountain Crow, Paunch Indians and the River Crow, the Raven Indians. Lewis and Clark recorded the Crow Indian's population in 1804.

In 1805, Lewis and Clark sat on a blanket to trade with the Nez Perce, who said they did not want red beads, but pale blue donut shaped beads, "a piece of the sky" they had obtained from the Spanish explorers early on.

Lewis and Clark heard blue Padres called "chief beads, "in the Nez Perce tongue or chief of all beads. The Nez Perce had received the blue padres earlier, most likely from Spanish explorers.

Before the white man, coastal Indians devised a monetary system called wampum. A mussel shell was broken into pieces by a stone hammer and each bead was rounded by abrasion.

A hole was drilled in the center using a bow-drill. The beads were strung on a leather thong and worn around the neck. Wampum was exchanged in trade creating a crude monetary system. The Indians had established a value for a bead strand called bead money.

Crow Medicine Chief
(Photograph Courtesy of Azusa Publishing, LLC)

Ships brought cowry shell, dentillium and marine hair-pipe from England. Barrel, conical, discoidal, flat, ovate, rectangular, round, spherical, truncate, and tubular shell were shipped in for the fur trade. Shell was cut and drilled for wampum beads. Other materials arrived, such as copper, gold and silver.

Glass beads from Europe gave the Crow beautiful manufactured beads to sew on leather clothing. Larger colorful glass beads were strung into gorgeous necklaces for trade or personal use. Beaded arm bands, earrings and necklaces were worn for adornment.

The "Crow Bead" is a donut shaped glass trade bead about 3/16 inch in height and 5/8 inch in diameter more than twice the size and thickness of the pony bead. It was the favorite bead of the Crow Indians, named for them. Traders said the Crow demanded the beads.

When the white traders arrived and built trading posts, Indians could obtain clothing and blankets made of cloth. In addition, Indians traded furs for glass beads, steel knives and firearms.

The firearms introduced to the Crow were "big medicine and a mystery." Bone, hair-pipe and shell were used in the fur trade with the Indians.

Fort Lisa was established by Manuel Lisa of the Missouri Fur Company in 1809 between the mouth of the Little Missouri and the Big Knife Rivers in Crow territory in what is now North Dakota.

The Pierre and Marie Dorion family departed St. Louis with the Hunt Party and embarked up the Missouri in dugout canoes, reaching an Arikara Indian village in 1811 and cached their canoes. Hunt bartered with the Arikara and Crow Indian traders for horses and crossed over the looming Bighorn Mountains to the Wind River

44

in just eighteen days. Again Hunt traded for new mounts with the Cheyenne Indians, trade partners of the Arikara. They crossed Union Pass to the Green River Valley and traded jerky from the Shoshoni.

The party hunted buffalo and jerked nearly two tons of meat. They crossed the Hobart River Valley and reached the Snake River. and decided against dugouts.

They rode horses across the Continental Divide southwest to Jackson's Hole and hiked out of the Teton Range. Four traders remained to trap beaver, near Three Forks, in the spring of 1812. The Crow killed one of the trappers.

About the age of 20, braves joined the clans. In the Crow Nation, there were thirteen clans in the exogamous rule of matrilineal descent grouped together, loosely.

Some of the clans were the Bad War Honors, Crows, Filth-Eating Lodge, Greasy-Inside-the-Mouth, Kicked-in-Their-Bellies, Lumpwoods, Newly-Made Lodges, Piegan Lodge, Sore-Lip Lodge, Streaked Lodge, Thick Lodge, Tied-In-a-Knot, Treacherous Lodge, Whistling Water, and Without-Shooting-They-Bring-Game.

Plenty Coups joined the Sore-Lips clan. The clan was a brotherhood and treated members as brothers and wives as sisters. A clan brother could dance with one's wife and they exchanged gifts.

The clan was important to the Crow culture and a life way. Membership in a clan was matrilineal. One is born into the clan of the natural mother.

Blood relatives joined the clan for life with a close sense of kinship. Crow clansmen were active in war, sports and life. Clans-people were required to marry outside of the clan and not a family member. The clan system ranked higher than family. Their priority was the clan before the tribe.

A dying father left his horses and possessions to his wife or other relatives, but in Crow inheritance, a man left property to a brother clansman, like his own family. Objects were left to a clan brother's children instead of the family. The medicine bundle, pipe and Sun Dance doll were inherited. Members of the clan stole wives of rival members as sport and claimed to have slept with one of their wives. If she called the claimant a liar, she could escape capture or follow him to his lodge.

Clan members became camp police during the camp move. Duties rotated between societies. Headmen were picked for valor in battle or hunt savvy. A camp chief directed camp moves.

The hunt leader directed their activity. The war chief led in battle. A group acted as police on the hunt and scourged those, who hunted the herd early, broke weapons or took game illegally. Murder was avenged by putting the murderer to death creating feuding in the clans. A killer compensated the family of the victim.

The Crow society was a men's lodge with its own name and ceremonial lodge. The society held its own dances, celebrations and festivities. The societies were similar in association. Crow societies were not graded and membership was voluntary. Societal groups were small, having ten-twenty members; some societies had sixty. A warrior belonged to one society for life. A great warrior could join more than one society, but Crow women could not join a man's society. The lodge was painted with symbols; societies had names, medicine bundles and insignias. There was rivalry over the first coup.

Crow Encampment
(Photograph Courtesy of Azusa Publishing, LLC)

Other militant Plains societies were called Big Dogs, Bull's, Foxes, Kit-foxes, and Ravens. The Crow Foxes were elected for the summer and carried curved staffs with otter fur. Two officers carried straight staffs adorned with eagle feathers. One staff bearer carried his staff and inserted it into the ground throughout the battle.

One of the greatest leaders of the Crow Nation was Arapooash, who was born after the split. Chief Arapooash was a successful war chief in battle. He led war parties against the Arikara, Assiniboine, Atsina, Blackfoot, Cheyenne, Flathead, Nez Perce and Sioux and has been called the greatest Crow war chief.

Born after 1800, Sore Belly was a great leader of the River Crow Nation. Sore Belly was a war chief, who succeeded *Arapooash*. Sore Belly was a holy man, medicine man and prophet.

As a young chieftain, Sore Belly led 400 warriors on the war path against the Blackfoot Indians. His Crow scouts spied on the village before the raid. The chief assembled his warriors at night ready to attack at dawn; the war party caught the Blackfoot off guard. Outnumbered, they had heavy losses with 100 dead. The Crows counted 22 dead.

Years earlier, a Cheyenne war party massacred a band of 30 Crow lodges, while Sore Belly returned from visiting the Flathead He retaliated by leading 600 warriors on the war trail. They caught the Cheyenne at the Arkansas at daybreak, and stampeded their horses.

They surrounded the camp and ambushed them. They had no avenue of escape. The fighting ceased; 200 Cheyenne lay dead and 300 women and children taken captive and 1,000 horses. On the trek home, Crow warriors contracted smallpox from the captives or from immigrants and brought the dreaded disease to their village; one of six lived and escaped into the mountains.

In 1825, Crow Chief Long Hair and Major O'Fallon of the U.S. Army signed a friendship pact between the Crow Nation and the United States. Chief Rotten Tail refused to sign.

From 1840-1850, the Crow Indians contracted smallpox from the immigrants. With a population of 10, 000 in 1830, by 1850 it had dropped to roughly 2,000. At that time, Chief Sore Belly took measures to preserve his band. The enemy of the Crow people, the Blackfeet tribe's population was said to be 30,000 in 1834, but only 13,000 in 1850 due to smallpox.

Chief Sore Belly sent runners in all directions to round up any surviving members of the Crow tribe and found husbands and wives for them using the Cheyenne captives. He distributed horses, rifles and provisions among the survivors, saving his dying band.

Sore Belly raided a fur fort in Blackfoot Country on the Upper Missouri attacking the palefaces who had given them smallpox. The Crow war party had planned to capture ammunition, guns and horses. The Blackfoot Indians had migrated north to barter at the trading posts.

The Crow attacked the fort, but were held off by the fur trappers. Sore Belly said previously if they could not capture the fort, he would leave his body in the Land of the Blackfoot.

When they came back Sore Belly took his own life. The River Crow returned to the mountains and never followed the war trail again. It was customary for a band to move after the death of a chief.

Between 1800 and 1840, the glass pony bead was a popular bead traded was traded to the Indians. The pony bead was donut shaped, a little larger than the pound bead. The glass pony bead came from Venice and was introduced to the American Indians. The fur trader brought beige, black, blue red and white beads for trade.

Two stories are told to explain the name, "pony bead." The first story has nearly become a folk tale. During the fur trade with the Indians a strand of beads 3/8 inch in diameter by eight feet long traded for a pony back then, thus the name pony bead.

The other rendition was that Russian merchants used small Tartar ponies to transport their bead stock across the Bering Straits. Here we have another clue for the name, pony bead.

Either theory could apply. Around 1840, the colorful glass seed bead was introduced to the American Indian tribes. Seed beads are around 1/16 inches in diameter, some smaller; cut beads were quite popular.

In 1851, a band of River Crow under Chief Rotten Tail arrived at Fort Union to trade wearing beautifully painted buffalo robes with symbols of hunting and war and adorned with glass beads and quillwork.

The Crow Indians were famous for their beautifully painted robes. The gorgeous robes had bows, buffaloes, guns, horses, human figures, scalp-locks and various illustrious symbols of war were painted on them in bright colors.

Their buffalo robes were popular for trade with other tribes and used as outer garments. They were worn as fine warm articles of clothing.

CHAPTER FOUR
CROW HORSES

The Crow Indians went through a long evolution from the Great Lakes region west to the Great Plains. The walking Indians migrated westward and spilled onto the Great Plains of present day southern Montana and eastern Wyoming to hunt the buffalo (pte), in the Crow dialect.

Buffalo are wild cattle that grazed in herds foraging for greener pastures eating prairie grasses down to the roots. The Crow first hunted buffalo as walking Indians and were hunters and gatherers who toted goods on their backs and utilized dog travois to carry their wares. Travois dogs hauled wood extensively. Crow women trained the dogs and selected them for the task.

They could only kill a small number of bison in a short time, before the herd moved on foraging for food. The whole camp moved as the bison migrated nonstop in the spring, summer and fall.

Crow nomads moved their tents and goods with the herd every few days. Squaws pitched camp, while the braves hunted the buffalo. Small bands pursued buffalo at subsistence levels. Crow lived in scattered camps across the prairie.

French trappers called the Dakota the "Sioux," a corruption of the Siouan language. With the help of horses and firearms, the Sioux pushed the Crow farther west into present day North and South Dakota and onto the Great Plains. The Sioux contested the Crow buffalo hunting grounds. When the Crow Indians gained horses and firearms, they could fight the Sioux without the disadvantage of battling on foot.

51

Mandans maintained a trade center as trade partners with the Crow and Hidatsa, who formed the hub of trade on the Upper Missouri. Crow traders carried goods and criss-crossed the northwest from major trade centers of the Arikara, Cheyenne, Hidatsa, Mandan and Shoshoni Indians. They serving as middlemen between the Eastern Shoshoni trade center in present day southwestern Wyoming and the Mandan–Hidatsa and Arikara trade centers in what is now North and South Dakota. They bartered flintlock, musket and pistol trade guns.

American Indians lived on the land for thousands of years prior to the modern horse. Wild horses like zebras, once roamed free in America. Theory is that they were a food source and not ridden.

Cortez brought the first horses in the 16th Century to America. Ute Indians stole horses and were the first Indians to acquire them. Ute Indians called horses, "big dogs," never having seen one and thought them to be like elk. Cortez imprisoned Utes for horse theft and forced them to work in the gold and silver mines.

Apaches raided the colonists in the late 1600's and stole horses. Counting coup, Comanche Indians stole in at night and took horses from the Apaches. Although the Comanche obtained the horse late, they became the most expert horsemen and the fiercest warriors of the Southern Plains. Comanche horsemen chased Ute hunting buffalo on the plains, scared them off, and scattered their camps. They stole mustangs in northern Mexico, New Mexico and Texas ranchos.

Spaniards were tyrannical slave masters and treated their slaves very badly, scourging them. The Navajo and other slaves rose up and rebelled against the evil Spaniards. During the Pueblo Revolt

Appaloosa Horse
(Photograph Courtesy of Jumper Horse/Sport)

in 1680, many horses broke free and roamed the desert. Others were captured and driven north from the Pueblos.

All Apache and Ute Indians had horses. Comanche Indians caught wild mustangs with a lasso, broke and gentled them. The Indian technique of breaking horses began by holding the horse with lassoes. The horse was jerked off its feet barely breathing, as the noose tightened restricting its air supply, as it lay there gasping for air. The lasso was relaxed and the horse rose, weak and trembling. Its ears, forehead and nose were stroked. The Indian blew into its nostrils, bridled the mustang, mounted it and rode away.

Comanche horse Indians traded ponies with the Apache and Ute Indians in the southwest and built up their stock and amassed thousands of ponies in horse wealth. A warrior owned as many as 250 horses and a chief could possess a herd of over 1,000 horses.

The Comanche Indians were responsible for populating the Pacific Northwest with horses. In the early 1700's, Comanche horsemen drove thousands of ponies north from present day Texas to their Northern Shoshoni counterparts in what is now Idaho and Wyoming. Many northern tribes received horses from the Comanche.

Circa 1725, the Crow Indians first obtained horses from a Shoshoni Indian camp on the Green River near the Great Salt Lake, and herded them back to the Upper Wind River Valley, all in present day Wyoming.

When the Crow returned to the Upper Wind River with horses, the band was inquisitive, never having seen these creatures. A man stood next to a horse and was kicked in the gut. The name stuck and a Crow band named themselves, the "Kicked in Their Bellies."

54

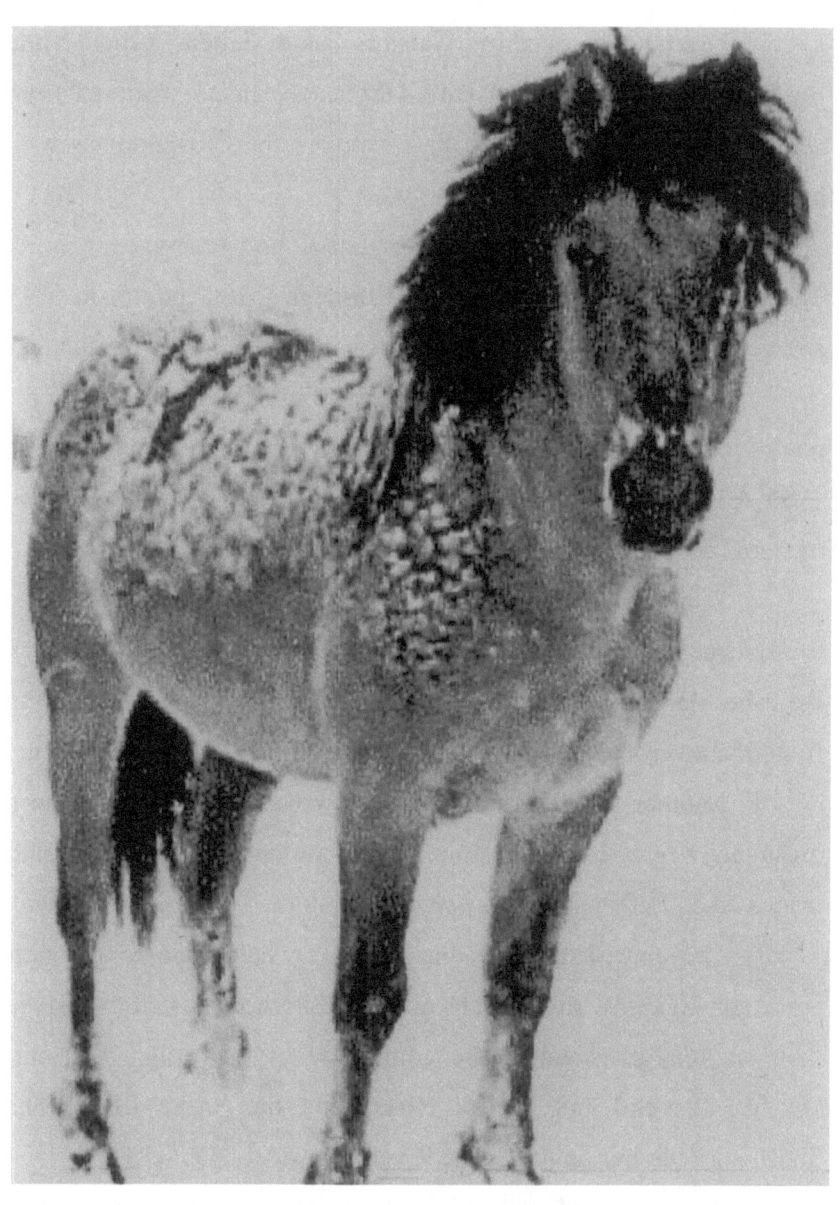

Spanish Mustang Buffalo Horse
(Photo courtesy of www.aaanativearts.com)

Legend told of Crow warriors led by Young Chief White Buffalo, who obtained steel knives from the Hidatsa bartered from white traders. White Buffalo first supplied the Crow Indians with horses.

The Crows saw the need for horses and returned for more. The Hudson's Bay Company passed through Crow country in 1745 and noted the Crows had lots of horses and provided fresh mounts.

The Blackfeet Indians traded the Comanche horse Indians for ponies, circa 1745 A.D. and the Crow received horses from them in 1760 A.D. This was the beginning of the "Horse Culture." The modern horse became a type of savior of the Crow Indians.

With Shoshoni and Comanche horses, the Crow began to breed them and to build up their herds. A large herd showed status in the tribe. Horse wealth made bride price. Twenty horses tied up in front of a lover's teepee might be accepted by the fair Indian maiden.

Another account told how a Crow warrior saw a horse in a dream and began to seek the animal. He saw several horses emerging from a lake. He caught a few horses and returned to camp with them.

Cheyenne, Kiowa, Mandan and Crow held trade fairs in their horse complexes. Crow Indians attended Shoshoni-hosted trade-fairs held on a large island at the confluence of the Boise, Malheur, Owyhee, Payette and Weiser Rivers and the Snake River. The Shoshoni trade-fair on the Snake River was widely publicized.

Peaceable Indians, even enemy tribes, were welcomed if they came in peace. Tribes were welcomed from far and wide to join in the celebration, dancing, gambling, and trading arrow heads, arrows, bows, horses, knives, lodge-poles, pelts, and other items. The Wind

River Shoshoni also held trade-fairs in western Wyoming. Horse trading was good commerce and it also created good will.

The Nez Perce and Palouse Indians bartered and bred Appaloosa horses which were their favorite breed, probably mostly acquired from the Comanche Indians. Horses diffused to various tribes throughout the northwest from the Shoshonis trade fairs held in present day Idaho. Crows, Flatheads and Nez Perce came to trade.

The Rocky Mountain Fur Company traded with the Crow. Crow Indians bartered horses, bridle-bits, and blankets to the Shoshoni for guns and ammunition. With horses and guns, the Crow's buffalo hunting improved.

Charles Mackenzie observed the Hidatsa Indians on the Missouri trading with the Plains Crow in 1805. Three hundred Crow Lodges of Indians arrived at the Hidatsa village to trade and smoked the pipe of friendship.

The Hidatsa opened trading with hundreds of weapons and rounds of ammunition plus axes, goods, kettles, and 100 bushels of Indian corn as gifts for the Crow. The Crow countered with gifts of 250 horses, buffalo jerky, robes, leggings and war shirts.

In 1806, on their return trip to St. Louis, Lewis and Clark lost horses when Crow warriors took ponies belonging to the party from Nathaniel Pryor.

With horses, the Crow Indians became Plains Indians and with the buffalo utilized the tipi. They rode horses that drug travois, hauled goods, moved their camps, gave them a means to hunt, and go to war and became excellent horse handlers, raisers and fine horsemen.

Sioux forced the Crows off their hunting grounds along with other tribes. The Crow objected highly to the Sioux claiming Powder River Country, Crow hunting grounds.

Other tribes, who wanted to hunt buffalo in Crow territory, were pushed off the hunting grounds. The Sioux and Cheyenne claimed the Crow tribe's lands and took the best hunting grounds. Several tribes were forced to share the land.

Blackfeet Indians attacked the Cree on horseback on the Saskatchewan and the Crow on the Yellowstone, 1840-1850. The River Crows, aided by Gros Ventre allies, were driven south across the Missouri by the Assiniboine, Blackfeet, Cree and Yankton Sioux.

James P. Beckwourth was a black mountain man, who signed on as a blacksmith and indentured servant with a fur trading expedition in 1824 into the Rockies and stayed on as a fur trapper. He stayed in the Rockies and lodged with the Blackfoot and married the daughter of the chief.

He later married a Crow woman in 1830 and lived with the Crow Indians becoming one of them and even becoming a head chief. In 1855, His son became chief of the Crow Nation. Jim died in 1866 and was interred in a tree platform burial.

The horse provided their transportation and provided many a good horse race. Indians loved horses. They painted ponies for war with hand prints and designs; feathers and ribbons were tied to their manes and tails.

The Crow crafted men's and women's Indian saddles. The pad saddle was popular with them, made of two leather pieces, sewn together and stuffed with either feathers or grass. The frame saddle of

Plainswoman, Horse & Travois
(Photograph Courtesy of Azusa Publishing, LLC)

bison bone, wood or deer antler was lightweight with wet rawhide stretched over it, shrunk to size, attached by a single cinch of hair.

The bridle was made of horse hair, stitched about the horse's jaw. They used leather bridals, stirrups, reins and Indian saddle blankets. Bridles, saddles and pommels were heavily beaded.

Saddles were adorned with saddle blankets and supple folds of buffalo hide. Trade blankets also made fine saddle blankets. Trade blankets were also used. Buffalo skins and mountain lion skins edged in bright red cloth were used for saddle blankets.

The mountain lion is called the catamount, cougar, painter, panther, and puma. It has relatively short, tawny colored hair and has been referred to as the "Ghost of the Rockies." The big cat gets its name because it is so seldom seen by humans, lives primarily in caves up high in the mountains and normally hunts at night. Mature adults measure three feet in height by five feet in length.

Crow horsemen adorned their ponies with colorful beaded aprons, bridal straps, head ornaments, horse collars. They roached pony's manes and notched the ears of buffalo and war horses. Beaded ornaments were attached to the horses' foreheads. Buffalo head masks with horns were employed for horses' head gear.

Their culture centered on the buffalo, horse and warfare. Crow bands of nomadic hunters, who followed the bison onto the Plains as they grazed continually ate down the grasses and constantly moved.

Consequently, the Crow bands pursued the migrating herds. The whole camp followed the bison and the hunters went out on their best buffalo horses and singled out buffalo for the kill.

The Nez Perce raised Appaloosas
(Courtesy of Jumper Horse/Sport)

The scouts determined the herd's location and approached downwind to not frighten the grazing bison that sensed their presence. Extra horses were taken on the hunt. Pack horses hauled meat and skins. In war, warriors left fresh horses tethered near the battle scene.

Hunting or warring Crow warriors mostly rode bareback. A good war horse doubled as a fine buffalo horse. Bison were hunted on horseback (buffalo runners).

They followed bison herd movements or rode far to reach the buffalo. The Crow excelled in hunting the buffalo and were skilled buffalo hunters on horseback. Buffalo provided needed meat, clothing, and teepee coverings.

The hunt chief gave a war whoop and the buffalo stampeded; the chase was on. The hunter rode his best buffalo horse alongside a grunting buffalo in flight, penetrating his tough outer skin with a well aimed arrow behind the last rib and struck its lungs.

On moonlit nights Crow war parties made raids on enemy camps to take horses and brought extra moccasins along. Stealing horses from other tribes was called taking coup.

One horse stolen counted as a coup and brought much honor. The Crow Indians rode long distances to reach enemy camps in order to take horses. Braves stole quietly into enemy camps, and cut the reins to take horses.

The Crow became some of the finest Indian horsemen on the Plains. Crow warriors could compete with any Plains Indians. They went on the warpath to steal ponies and the Crow took many ponies. They fought the toughest tribes with valor. The Crow warrior was a match for the Sioux and Blackfeet Indians.

CHAPTER FIVE
PLAINS CROW

The Cheyenne and Sioux drove the Crow westward. They moved onto the Plains getting the horse around 1700 A.D. Intertribal warfare increased when the Plains Indians gained horses. The Crow men constantly fought battles and raided for horses. Crow Indian warriors became a skilled fighting unit against enemy tribes. The Crow combated the Blackfeet, Sioux and took many scalps and raided for more ponies.

The Crow warriors held off the Arapahoe, Cheyenne and Sioux, when outnumbered 10 to one in 1864 near present day Pryor, Montana and proved to be one of the strongest tribes on the Plains.

Crow warriors prepared to go on a war party by performing the war dance. The dance was to build their courage and give them power. The antics and movements of the war dance mimicked the actual war with the enemy before going on the war trail. A victory dance followed the actual battle. Plains Indian artists used basic painting techniques, but produced beautiful results. Paint dishes were crafted from thin slabs of stone hollowed into a dish. A crude paint brush was devised from a pointed bone making the tiniest brushes.

Paint was made from natural pigments of colors: black, blue, brown, green, red, white and yellow of crushed stone and soil. Yellow soil was found along the Yellowstone. Berries made paint. Paint was applied with the finger tips to apply streaks on the face with blue, green, red, and yellow colors   painted vertically and horizontally.

Bodies and faces were painted regularly to go to war. A pointed bone or stick was used to apply paint down the center. The

63

fingers were first dipped into bear grease or buffalo back fat and then inserted into a powdered pigment. Three fingers were used to apply the war paint to the face and also the body. Crow men smeared bear-grease on their bodies to protect their skin from exposure to insects, sun and wind.

The Crow warriors fought for revenge of a lost skirmish or of a brother or friend. They raided for horses to retaliate for horses stolen from them and were in a constant state of war.

A Crow warrior had to meet four demands before being considered for chief. He had to take coup and also wrest a weapon from an enemy and also had to go on a night raid and steal a horse (coup) and it was imperative the warrior had led a successful raid.

There were three famous female chiefs in the Crow nation. In 1800, Comes-Toward-the-Near-Bank and her husband, Knife were war-chiefs. Woman Chief was a Crow leader in the early 1800's and in 1830, Pine Leaf led a raid killing four Blackfeet and made chief. Women seldom went on the war trail.

Trappers formed alliances with the Crow, Flathead and Shoshoni Indians and opened up trade with them. The Blackfeet tried to stop white trappers from invading their territory. Fur traders, John Coulter and George Druillard trapped for the Manual Lisa Company on the Missouri and Yellowstone and traded with the Crow.

Early western artist, George Catlin visited a Crow village in the 1830's and commented on the expediency of the squaws in disassembling teepees in a matter of minutes and how they could be moved and transported over the Plains, easily and how they pitched teepees in a groove of trees for shelter from the cold.

Buffalo Hunting Bareback
Len Sodenkamp, Boise Artist

Catlin observed how the Crow made one type of shelter from crude logs, similar to a Lemhi Shoshoni long house from saplings. Catlin marveled as he watched warriors hunt buffalo and observed women as they dressed out the skins. He noted how expediently they jerked and ground pemmican, making cakes of berries and tallow.

In 1833, the Crow killed 200 Cheyenne. That year, they contracted smallpox from the wagon trains.

Jesuit Father De Smet began his life work among the Indians in 1840, when he trekked into the Rockies of now Idaho and visited the Flathead and Pend d' Oreille Indians. On his return trip he called on the Crow, Gros Ventres, and other tribes of Indians traveling hundreds of miles. The next year, the priest returned to the Flatheads administering the Christian religion. He and Father Nicholas Point established St. Mary's Mission on the Bitterroot, south of Missoula.

In 1840, the Comanche Indians of the Southern Plains, sat with the Arapahoe and Cheyenne and smoked the pipe of peace. The Comanche gifted their new allies with a great number of horses.

In 1846, the Crow massacred a Piegan Blackfeet band of Small Robes. In 1848, they caught smallpox again, this time from the Northern Shoshoni and in 1849, nearly 600 Crow died of influenza. The Crow tribe was well represented in 1851 at Fort Laramie.

The fort was surrounded by Sioux Indian tipis when Father De Smet arrived. The priest was highly loved and respected by the Indians and sat at the peace table on the Treaty council. Smoke wisped out of the openings. Children ran and played as dogs barked. Horses and mules grazed on the prairie grasses. Indians clustered in groups as the women worked. Others conducted trade.

66

Father De Smet

The government designated mountain man, Thomas "Broken Hand" Fitzpatrick to initiate a plan to remove tribal borders to prevent warfare over lands between tribes in 1851 at Fort Laramie. The Fort Laramie Peace Treaty identified 38.5 million acres on the Upper Yellowstone as Crow lands in 1851, Crow Chief, Big Robber signed.

In the "Horse Culture Era," the Crow were in their glory. They gathered a huge surplus of horseflesh as wealth in horses. They acquired the horse and became equestrian buffalo hunters as Plains Indian tribes. Warriors bred and raised enough horses to hunt buffalo, for trade, and to go to war. They loved the buffalo hunt on horseback.

The Mountain and River Crow bands had found their forte on the Plains. They formed buffalo hunting societies like many other Plains Indian peoples and lived on the buffalo. Their place was on horses hunting the buffalo.

Colonel Carrington called a formal council at Fort Phil Kearny with the Cheyenne chiefs, allies of the Sioux, July 1, 1866. Carrington asked Chief Black Horse why the Sioux claimed Crow lands and was told, they took the best hunting grounds. The Cheyenne conceded the land to the Crow.

The Crow people believed the buffalo was created especially for them. They depended on the buffalo primarily for the meat and hides. They jerked the meat and made pemmican.

Their goods were crafted from the buffalo bones, hides, and horn. The meat was top-grade and they were living at the top of the food-chain. The Buffalo horns and hooves were used in ceremonies. The Crow depended on the buffalo for clothing, lodging, robes, sustenance, and bi-products.

Bull buffalo normally fought for rites to breed the herd. Bellowing, battling, the bigger dust cloud, the more impressive was the bull. They waged fierce battles facing off and butting horns. The stronger bull won mating privileges and the females of the herd.

Wolfs run in packs except the "lone wolf," the omega wolf driven from the pack. The lone wolf could get a reprieve if he found a mate to start a new pack. The alpha pair led the pack in everyday life and the hunt and the chase to down an elk or other prey for food. Wolves live communally in packs. Offspring are born into the pack.

Wolf packs trailed the herd waiting for a young or weak buffalo to savagely attack for a feast. It was common to see a single wolf near them, but a pack of wolves was a threat.

The buffalo were accustomed to just one wolf, so a hunter could crawl among the herd beneath a wolf skin and was able to fire arrows and kill a buffalo.

Raven scavengers have a symbiotic relationship with wolves and follow wolf packs in order to feed on the same carcass. Wolves sometimes watch for circling ravens in order to help share the carcass.

One method of hunting buffalo on foot was to crawl among the herd beneath a buffalo skin. A trap was built in a "v" oft times on a hill as a corral. The hunter decoy moved away from the herd bleating like a baby calf. Buffalo have weak eyes and are rather dumb and a female invariably followed the bleating into the corral.

A "buffalo jump" was a cliff where lanes were built in advance to guide the buffalo along. The shaman started a fire or waved a blanket and shouted to stampede the herd over a cliff to their deaths.

Butchering stations were established below. Buffalo were skinned and the hides processed in warm water, hung from a branch, staked down driving pegs into the ground around the perimeter.

Buffalo skin was fleshed using stone hide scrapers to remove all of the waste. The hump was removed and the skin stitched with deer sinew, using bone awls and needles. The squaws chewed the leather for softening. Skins were also pounded with stone pounders to soften them and urine was used as an agent.

Brains were removed from the skulls and women processed the skins with the brain paste solution to soften and tan the hides and process the leather that made clothing, moccasins, and teepees. Stone hide beaters softened them more. The hides were cured and dried.

Hides were either scraped with stone hide scrapers or the fur side was left intact for comfort. Many buffalo hides were left intact with the thick fur and used for warm robes worn in cold weather. They wore the robes like a blanket around them. Crow robes were of the finest quality leather. Both braves and squaws wore buffalo robes. Tanned buffalo hides were bone white and made a good surface for paint.

A group of chiefs sitting in a circle in buffalo robes appeared to be buffalo. They believed in a symbolic transfer of power from the buffalo and a sacred bond between a woman and the buffalo.

Buffalo skins were decorated with painted ornate symbols of hunting and war signified position in the tribe of political and social order. Bear, buffalo and rabbit skins made clothing, and robes. The Crows were renowned for their most beautiful beadwork and gorgeous quillwork.

Sioux chiefs at 1851 Fort Laramie Peace Treaty,
Left to right: Spotted Tail, Roman Nose, Old-Man-Afraid-of His-
Horses, Lone Horn, Whistling Elk, Pipe and Slow Bull, not shown.
(Photograph Courtesy of Azusa Publishing, LLC)

Father De Smet was contacted to return to Fort Laramie; he served on the council of the Fort Laramie Treaty of 1868 with the Plains Indians that reduced the Crow reservation to 8 million acres. The Black Robe priest earned the esteem of hundreds of American Indians and contributed to peace in the West. The Laramie Treaty established the Crow reservation in Montana and divided the Sioux into hostile or reservation Indians led by Sitting Bull.

A Crow Agency was opened in 1869 on Hide Scraper Creek. By 1870, the Crow were expected to transition onto the reservation. In 1872, the Agency was moved to Absarokee, Montana.

In 1871, Congress passed a law that nearly caused extinction of the buffalo by ordering all bison killed to force all Indians onto reservations. Bison were needlessly slaughtered for their tongues and skins, the carcasses left to rot. Bison became scarce on the Plains; buffalo grazing land cut in half. Their numbers reduced by three-fourths; by 1900, buffalo were scarce, only 3 million on the Plains.

Hunters traveled to the Upper Missouri to find buffalo. An abundance of bison had existed on the Snake River Plain westward into what is now Oregon to the base of the Blue Mountains, but the herds were gone due to over-kill.

They say 50,000,000 buffalo once roamed the plains within a huge triangle between Great Bear Lake, Canada south to Mexico and eastward along the Appalachians.

The Plains Crow were mostly nomadic following the buffalo. Other bands lived in villages and grew beans, corn, squash and some tobacco, as semi-nomadic hunters. They hunted antelope, deer, and elk with bow and arrows, sharing their kill with poor Crow families.

72

American Bison
Author Photo

They trapped and hunted animals for pelts for trade. Crows did not eat puppies, and complained of boney fish.

After the hunt, they had a traditional feast. Women served buffalo tongue, berries, ribs, and pemmican. The Crow sat around the campfire and told stories of the hunt and war, a time for merriment. There were dances for men and for women.

One weapon utilized by the Crow Indians in hunting rabbits and other small game was the "rabbit stick." A rabbit stick was shaped similar to a boomerang and thrown to kill mostly rabbits.

Squaws did the lion's share of the work, tended teepees, raised children, and cooked; girls carried water and firewood. They dug roots, gathered fleshy plants, nuts and berries, during the "Moon of the ripe June-berries," camped near water to bath, cook and drink.

Crow women made the family's clothing. Squaws rubbed deer hides with brain paste mixed with liver soaked in water for several days and were wrung out, stretched, dried and softened. Deer skins were smoked to add color. Women used deerskin material to make dresses, leggings, loin cloths and moccasins, as did elk skins.

Styles of clothing designated position in the Crow tribe like the painted buffalo robe. Colors painted on a buffalo robe were blue for sky or water, red for sun, green for grass and trees.

Women wore robes with geometric designs; some men's robes had concentric circles of feathers in a sunburst to represent a war bonnet. Designs were also made with colorful trade beads and dyed porcupine quills. The painted skins were traded to other tribes.

The buckskin ceremonial war shirt was highly decorated. The war shirt was adorned on the arms and shoulders with brightly

Crow Woman Carrying Firewood
(Photograph Courtesy of Azusa Publishing, LLC)

colored stripes of blue, green, red, white and yellow beads, crosses and other symbols. The Crow had no written language, but used pictograph symbols. Painted designs on animal hides were common practice. Symbols on men's robes were mostly pictographs.

Dyed porcupine quill patterns were added. It was embellished with eagle feathers and human hair fringe. Special Crow garb took on a sacred nature worn by members of the council and designated socio-political leaders.

Plains Indians buffalo hunters dressed similarly. Warriors wore a fringed war shirt, loin cloth, leggings and moccasins as daily wear, on the hunt and in battle. During the winter the men were clad in shirt, leggings, moccasins and a buffalo robe.

Women wore dresses, leggings and moccasins and a warm buffalo robe. In full dress, the Crow men wore a war shirt, leggings and moccasins, fully beaded, fringed and painted, with dyed quills.

Men's leather clothing was beaded with symbols and women's clothing displayed designs, usually in buckskin or rawhide. Leggings were cut fancy with bead, paint and quill adornment. Both sexes wore the glass beads around their necks.

A favorite necklace was a long white glass elliptical bead in many strands around the neck. They adorned their clothing with beadwork, quillwork and blue, green, red and yellow paint for the dance. A small buckskin medicine bag was worn around the neck, and an eagle-bone whistle.

Sky-blue glass beads were produced in China in the 1700-1800's. Chinese ships met with Spanish Galleons in harbors with an interpreter to trade. Spanish ships sailed from Spain for the "New World" laden with the blue beads.

Padre beads came from Catholic priests, who gave the beads with crosses to the Indians as prayer beads. Padres were the most acclaimed trade-bead in America. Bead styles changed after 1870 and the modern style of beadwork came into design.

Translucent seed beads were introduced to the Crow Indians. The new styles in beading lasted until 1900. Crow squaws adorned clothing with colorful seed beads using either the lazy stitch or the over-lay stitch employed by most Plains tribes. Many patterns had four or five points. One favorite color bead they used was lavender.

Post 1900, bags, belts, dresses, gun cases, and knife sheaths were beaded colors and designs varied from tribe to tribe. In that respect, bead designs could be used to recognize tribes.

The Crow Indians tattooed both sexes. Squaws were usually tattooed between the chin and the lips. Warriors were mostly tattooed on the arms and the chest.

Women kept their hair cropped at the shoulders or longer and men grew hair long to their waists; they were quite a handsome race. Hair styles helped identify the tribe. Men and women grew their hair long, parted their hair in the middle and braided on the sides. Men wrapped their braids with two inch strips of blue or red trade cloth or with otter fur or wolf fur wrapped around them to add to their motif.

Hair was sometimes roached and separated on the crown of the head and spread out in a circle. Men's hair was braided on top of the head, worn in a scalp lock or coiled into a bun that hung on the forehead or back of the head with eagle feathers inserted into it. One Crow hairstyle for a warrior was full length hair to the ground with a stuffed crow worn on the back of the head. Sometimes a thin braid hung down from the forehead.

The Crow utilized bird feathers to fletch their arrows. They also adorned their hair with feathers. A complete war-bonnet or headdress was worn by a chief.

War bonnets were crafted using bald eagle feathers. Tubular headdresses were formed from a buckskin cap, bedecked with eagle feathers. Eagle feather war bonnets trailed to the ground to represent the back of the buffalo. Bonnets were distinctive one tribe.

Feathers were gained from live eagles. A natural pit was chosen, covered with branches and baited. The catcher hid in the pit. As the eagle swooped down for the bait, he grabbed its legs and wrung its neck. Eagle bones made excellent whistles.

Crow Indians kept live eagles in stick cages to supply feathers for adornment. They kept the magnificent birds like pets and used the eagle feathers mainly for headdresses and to fletch arrows. Hawks were kept caged in the same way for the same purpose. Feathers were symbolic as head wear for the American Indians and were worn almost exclusively.

Feathers were worn in the hair and on their clothing for adornment. Bird feathers were used to decorate bags, weapon sheaths and on weapons. The Indians actually made pillows using feathers.

Eagles served as a guide in visions and a good sign that stood for bravery and strength. Owls on the other hand were a bad omen to

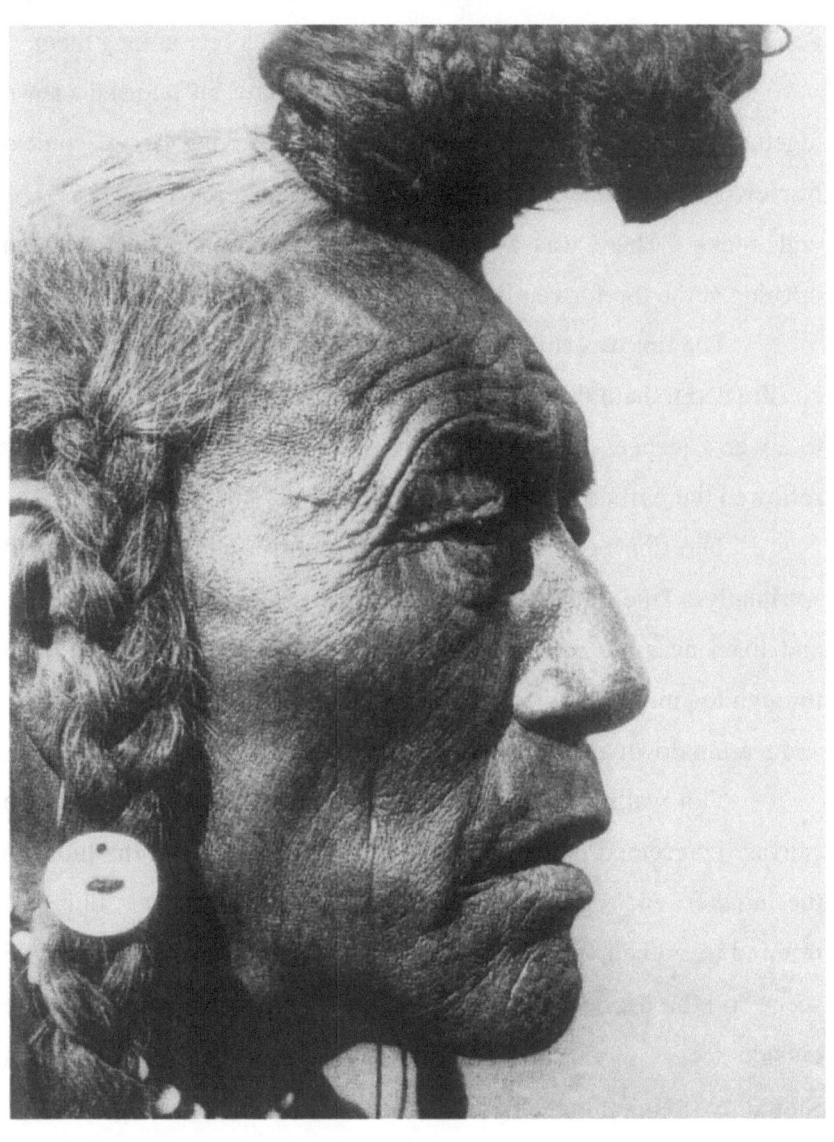

Crow Style Braid
(Photograph Courtesy of Azusa Publishing, LLC)

the Indians. If the Plains Indians had a dream or vision of an owl, it was a bad sign and foretold of death. Owls struck fear among them.

The Plains tipi (teepee) was a large tent of buffalo skins sewn together stretched over a number of lodge poles in a conical framework tied at the top with hide flooring, anchored at the base with rocks. There was a central hearth to cook and heat with an opening at the top for ventilation.

The tipi was collapsible and with two tipi poles, a travois was constructed to haul the tent and goods behind a horse laden with hides to cover a teepee, goods and infants. Women moved camp as they followed the buffalo. Travois poles were used in the tipi.

The tipi was the Crow woman's possession, physically and spiritually. Traditionally, the mother owned the tipi and its contents and lived near the wife's family and the lineage was passed down through the mother's line. Squaws had the responsibility of setting up and tearing down and were wife, mother of the children.

Tipi walls made from the white hide of the buffalo or white canvas represented purity to the Crow. Poles embraced the hide, as the mother encircles her children metaphorically. The tipi was referred to as their "second mother." It was traditional and contained scenes on the inside walls of the sun, moon and star gods and on the outside scenes of the brave's feats of the hunt and war. Tipi is a Siouan word meaning, "a place where one lives," or a wigwam.

The Crows paid a price befriending the palefaces, who gave them smallpox, took away their buffalo, land and demanded they live on reservations. Plenty Coups echoed the sentiment of the Indians'

Crow Princess
(Photograph Courtesy of Azusa Publishing, LLC)

loss of the buffalo. He described how the people faced starvation and their hearts fell on the ground and did not sing anymore.

Tobacco root grew wild or was planted. Historically, tobacco was traded at the forts. Secrets of the Tobacco Ceremony were passed down from. Clansmen feasted together.

When a member wanted to join the Tobacco Society, other clansmen chipped in and paid the enrollment expense. Male Crow Indians were chosen to join the Tobacco Society and were the only men in the village allowed to grow it. It was smoked socially and in sacred rituals. The clan performed religious tobacco ceremonies.

Tobacco in the Crow dialect was "ope." Bearberry leaves were mixed with tobacco. Medicine bundles, pipes and tobacco pouches were all sacred. Medicine bags were worn around the neck.

The ceremonial sacred pipe was smoked in peace and traditionally when going to war. Sacred pipes were stored in medicine bundles and contained sacred tobacco.

Crow women played a key role in helping their husbands handle the sacred medicine. Tobacco ranked high in the Crow tribe as a sacred object. Medicine was very important magic to the Crow people. Sacred medicine bundles, pipes, sun dance dolls, and tobacco bundles contained power.

The Crow cultivated tobacco; it also grew wild. It was planted ceremonially. The Hidatsa grew other tobaccos. Friends sat around the campfire as the host cut tobacco leaves to be smoked in a calumet pipe. Hand-crafted pipes were clay or stone. A mixture of tobacco, bearberry, leaves or a bark mixture was called kinnikinnick.

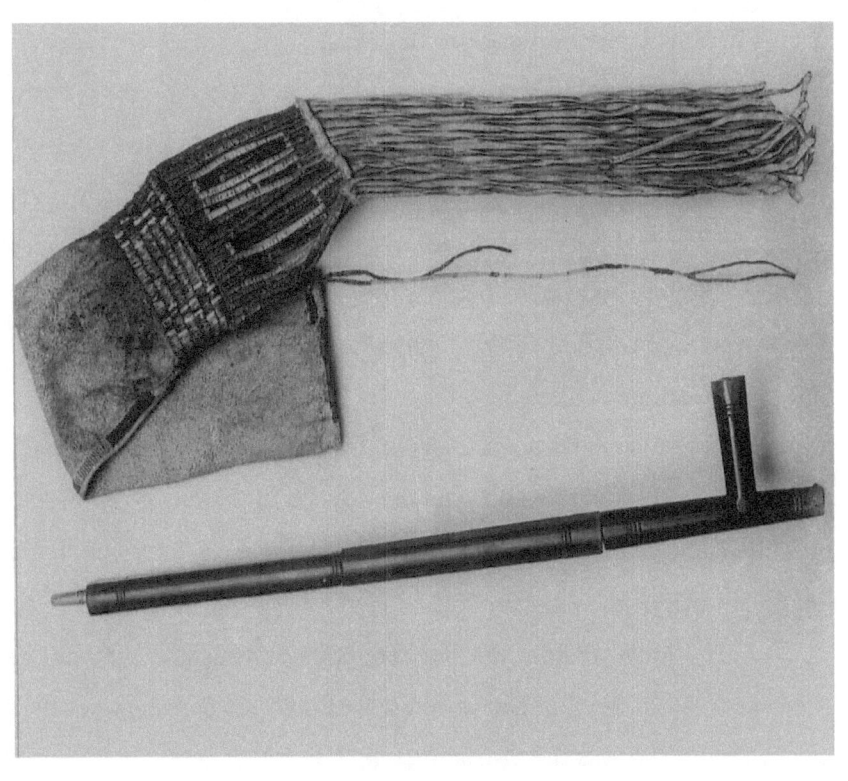

Calumet Pipe & Bag
(Photograph Courtesy of Idaho State Historical Society)

The Crow creator was referred to as the First Maker. Prayer to grandfather or *Wakan Tanka*, the source of their medicine and power and great mystery. A Crow shaman was called the "Wakan," which means medicine man. "Wakan" also meant sacred mystery.

The Native American Church movement was founded by Quanah Parker around 1890, among the Comanche Indians; it spread to other tribes, including the Crow Indians. Members used peyote cactus buttons in their divination.

Parker promoted the church and taught his people the "peyote road," led the Indians to Jesus Christ, through visions. The sacrament of the shaman was eating the cactus button, raw, portraying wolves eating the heart of the deer (creator).

Strength to win in battle came from strong medicine. The Crow were a prayerful people. Daily prayer to the Great Spirit was a duty. The Indian thanked his creator for life and prayed to the four directions, mother earth and the sky and was at one with nature.

The creator sun god was the source to power, growth, and warmth. They worshipped the sun god, source of their medicine and were truly sun worshippers.

The lodge builder ran the ceremony and made a vow as the sponsor to build the Sun Dance lodge and hold the dance, as revenge on an enemy and was the instructor.

The annual Sun Dance ranked above any during the year and was a time to worship their sacred god. Festivity was held in early summer during the full moon to let the creator's light shine on the world. The Sun was the most important ceremony of the Crow.

Sun Offering
(Photograph Courtesy of Azusa Publishing, LLC)

An altar was built in the lodge, painted buffalo skulls were laid on it. A coal on the altar was lit to burn through the night. The Mountain and River Crow celebrated the Sun Dance and held their own festivities of sacrifice and giving thanks,

In their time, the people put up their tipis surrounding the Sun lodge all around wearing their finest garb, on their best horses and all brought large quantities of food for the feast.   There was much merriment, singing and laughter and good times for all. Men sought purification in a sweat lodge, lamented, prayed and sang songs to the sun. A pledge for the recovery of the sick was offered. The Sun Dance Ordeal was portrayed in the movie, "A Man Called Horse."

Buffalo altars were used in Sun Dance Lodge. The Tobacco Order placed medicine bags on them for an offering. Animal droppings burned to light the sacred pipes and incense.

Sun Dance dolls were prepared with a piece of white-tail deerskin, white pine needles, hair from the temples and chin of a mountain sheep, a skunk skin necklace, buffalo skin rattle, hair-lock attachment and an eagle bone whistle all in a medicine bundle representing earth, mountains, rainbow and sky.

The warriors fasted and went without water and demonstrated feats of bravery before the Sun Dance and then entered the Sun Dance lodge to be purified and painted before the ceremony.

A tall cedar tree was chosen, cut down and trimmed for a center pole. The people gathered round and assisted dragging the sun pole to the site. A hole was dug and the pole uplifted and dropped into place; dirt was filled in around it. The medicine bundle and the Sun Dance doll were hung from the very top of the sun dance pole.

Self sacrifice involved self torture performed by the warriors in the evening, who danced around the sun pole (center pole) suspended by thongs fastened at the top of the pole to pegs inserted into slits in their chests for self affliction.

Crow dancers fasted and danced all night without water and mutilated themselves, rocked back and forth dancing to the throbbing beat of the drums.

Incantations were uttered. The warriors strained to tear the skin and free the skewers, or had them cut out at dawn by the dance leader, leaving scars for the rest of their lives. Squaws danced in the inner circle, but not around the sun pole

Buffalo skulls were inserted by thongs between the ropes and the pegs. They stared at the sacred medicine bundle or the Sun Dance doll as they danced. The dancers gazed at the bundle and prayed for power. The one who pledged the dance was given a Sun Dance doll by his mentor. The doll and sacred bundle were placed atop the pole.

The favorite Crow dance was the Sun Dance adopted from the Kiowa Sun dance medicine, (*taime*). As the dance drew to a close, there was a ceremony for chiefs to award new names to the warriors who earned them in battle.

New chiefs were chosen to replace those who retired. Sacred objects were wrapped and put up until the next Sun Dance, which ended with peace among the people.

The Sun Dance was practiced by most of the Plains tribes. The tribes of the Plains performing the Sun Dance were the Arapaho, Arikara, Blackfeet, Cheyenne, Hidatsa, Kiowa, Shoshoni, and Sioux Indians.

The all powerful medicine for a young brave achieving manhood was received through the vision quest. The adolescent brave ventured into nature for four days to receive see his vision and spirit guide (an animal or bird), for instance, an eagle, bear or cougar.

Cleansing, fasting, prayer and often mutilation were used to cause a hallucination. After severing a finger with his knife, the brave passed out, losing consciousness in an unconscious state and brave received his vision.

In matters surrounding death, the Crow Indians were greatly in fear of ghosts; if a close relative died they mourned and wailed and scarified their limbs with sharp stone or steel scalp knives.

Magic, divination, spells and trances were used for curing the sick. A medicine man foretold the hunt and events of war. He used drums, flutes, mariachis, rattles, and bone whistles for effect.

A deceased warrior's face was painted with his personal paint and symbols and he was dressed in his finest attire, with beautiful beaded moccasins and eagle feathers in his hair for burial. His bow, arrows, rifle, pipe, tobacco, fire making kit, and provisions for his long journey were all placed beside the body.

A fresh bison skin was wrapped around the body, tied with a leather thong. More skins were soaked in water and wrapped around the body to mummify it.

The prepared body was taken from the village to the burial site and hoisted up onto the burial platform. The whole ceremony was a very solemn occasion accompanied by wailing, beating of breasts and slashing of the limbs. The mutilation demonstrated mourning in loss of relation and close friendships.

Above-Crow Tree Burials   Below-Plains Burial Pyre
(Photographs Courtesy of Azusa Publishing,

The traditional Crow burial was the scaffold burial in close proximity to the village. Four upright poles were inserted into holes dug in the ground and four willows were tied to the poles to form a square platform with smaller willows cross-ways to support the body.

The Mandan Indians practiced the ritual of placing hundreds of human or buffalo skulls in a circle surrounding a scaffold burial eight or nine inches apart facing the center. The circle of skulls reached 20 or 30 feet in diameter.

Another type of burial was the tree platform burial, but the platform was built into the forks of very large tree branches. The deceased's horse was slaughtered and painted with large red blotches to show mourning. A Crow Indian burial grounds was sacred and not to be trespassed on. Crows believed evil spirits resided there.

Lodge burials were reserved for clan elites. The dead person's face was painted and he was dressed in his finest clothing, fancy beaded moccasins and adorned with his best strands of beads. They placed him on a bed with all of his personal possessions.

They believed that ghosts haunted places like this. Strangers were not welcome and it was wise for any other tribes or white men to make a wide berth around their Indian cemeteries.

The fierce Crow Indian tribes-people would track down and kill any enemy intruders that dared to trespass in the land of the dead.

In modern times, Archeologists have discovered the site of Indian graveyards in ill repair that are still partially standing. The American Indian tribes move and rebury all of the Indian cadavers that they can.

∧∧◇∧∧

CHAPTER SIX
LIVER-EATING-JOHNSON

This saga is the true story of the life of John Johnson, a Rocky Mountain fur trapper they called a squaw-man because he was married to a Flathead Indian woman. Johnson was a green horn when he traveled up the Missouri in 1843. As he bought his horse and trapping gear, Johnson was taken by a man named Robidoux, who charged him double for his horse and gear. The horse had been owned by a Comanche.

He met a trapper named John Hatcher, who became his trapping partner. They trekked into the Rocky Mountain, where Hatcher had his cabin in northwest Colorado. Hatcher offered Johnson one of his two Cheyenne Indian squaws for the winter, but he refused.

Johnson built a lean-to beside Hatcher's cabin, but Hatcher invited him to share the cabin and put the squaws in the lean-to and gifted him a tomahawk and taught him how to kill and scalp Indians.

As they began to trap there were no beaver left and other fur bearers had to be snared. Trapping with Hatcher, Johnson shot a grizzly bear twice; it stood up and charged him at close range. Hatcher shinnied up a tree as Johnson plunged a Bowie knife into the bruin's chest; the bear died.

In 1846, John Morgan, his wife, teenage daughter and young sons were traveling with a wagon train near Beatrice, Nebraska, when he got into an argument with the wagon-master. In anger, Morgan pulled out of the train. When he reached the Musselshell, Morgan put his oxen out to graze. He went to fetch them, but never returned.

Worried, his wife sent the boys to find him, then the daughter. When the girl screamed Mrs. Morgan grabbed an axe and ran after them. Her husband had been scalped by Blackfeet Indians and tied to a stake. The boys lay dead.

Their daughter lay naked on the ground dead; she had been raped and finally scalped. In shock and horror, Mrs. Morgan lost her mind. She killed the four warriors with the axe.

It was at that point that Johnson came along and helped her bury the family. She placed the heads of the four Blackfeet on stakes that Johnson had driven into each gravesite around the cabin to frighten any more marauding Indians away. Johnson built her a cabin.

Over time, he and Mrs. Morgan became close friends. Mountain men and trappers in the vicinity nicknamed her, "Crazy Woman." They left food at her door as charity. Living a solitary life, she gardened and hunted game.

In 1846, Johnson traded successfully with the Flathead Indians in the Wind River Range of Wyoming. Chief Bear's Head had offered him his daughter to be his bride, but Johnson refused.

Johnson's old partner, John Hatcher, quit trapping in 1847 and gave him his cabin and its furnishings and sent his Cheyenne wives back to their people; the Indian women walked away leading a pack horse. Hatcher remarked to Johnson, "watch your topknot," and headed west.

Bear's Head was pleasantly surprised when John Johnson returned with all kinds of gifts for the Flathead chief and his family as the bride-price for his daughter, with serious intentions of marrying The young woman called, "the Swan."

They parleyed and Johnson attended a roast dog feast. He brought bride-price of a rifle, two knives and some salt and vinegar for the chief's daughter; the Flathead chief accepted. So Johnson and Swan departed for the cabin on the Musselshell. On route, the bride put up their tent, made out a bed and cooked the evening meal.

In 1847, Johnson and his Flathead wife were going to have a child. While he was away conducting business, a Crow war party attacked their cabin. They murdered and scalped his wife, killing their unborn child.

Johnson vowed vengeance and purposefully humiliated the Crows for the death of his wife. He sought revenge using the old Bible adage "an eye for an eye and a tooth for a tooth."

Johnson was 6 foot 2 inches tall, 240 pounds, and had a muscular build. For awhile Johnson carried a Walker Colt and a Bowie knife and later wielded a tomahawk and a .45 Army Colt.

Johnson's horse was a huge black stallion and a sturdy mount. It scented Indians and would warn his master. The steed did not allow anyone near him except Johnson. John Johnson became a legend feared by the Crow. He was a fierce Indian fighter.

They said, he could kill a man with his bare hands by snapping his neck and one time Johnson killed four warriors with his fists and was deadly with his feet. Del Gue said that he had witnessed Johnson kill two Indians at once by kicking them.

Losing his family drove Johnson mad. He had a vendetta to live out and went after the Crow Indians in retaliation. Jonson was relentless in his pursuit and was feared by the Crow. They called him "Crow Killer," in their tongue, "Dapiek Absaroka."

He killed and scalped the Crow and he ate their livers raw, whether truth or fiction. Mountain men called him, "Liver-Eating Johnson." Indians believed if a warrior ate an enemy's heart, he gained his power.

Johnson became associated with famous Rocky Mountain trappers, like "Bear Claw" Chris Lapp, Bill Williams, and Del Gue. This is where Johnson gained a lot of trapping experience.

Bear Claw Chris Lapp had trapped with Bill Sublette. He made necklaces from grizzly bear claws and that was his trademark. His nickname was Bear Claw and he was famous for his necklaces.

Johnson became a target. His old trapping partner, Del Gue trapped with him in the 1850-60's. He rode with Johnson to Crazy Woman's cabin and saw him kill 20 Crow warriors who sought him.

The Crow honored Crazy Woman's cabin like a sacred Indian burial ground. They gave her cabin a wide berth and left her alone. It was the Crow's respect for Crazy Woman's cabin that finally ended Johnson's vendetta and he regained his sanity. He went back to trapping and hunting game as he had before and resumed the life of a respectable mountain man.

The story of Johnson spread across the west. The story of "Liver-Eating-Johnson" was repeated over open campfires and in the cabins of mountain men for decades. They told yarns and sang songs of Johnson's life. The mountain man's saga soon became legend.

Johnson became a famous figure of the "Old West." The legendary American frontiersman, John Johnson died in 1900. The movie, "Jeremiah Johnson" is a historic fiction film based on the life of the celebrated mountain man.

CHAPTER SEVEN

FORTS IN CROW COUNTRY

The Corps of Discovery built temporary forts as they trekked across America. In 1805, Lewis and Clark noted that the confluence of the Missouri and the Yellowstone was a good site for a trading post. Lewis discovered the Marias River. He traveled up the Marias to Cut Bank. Fort Piegan was later established there.

They constructed Fort Clapsop, which was named for local Indians on the south shore of the Columbia River. The structure was built of logs, after reaching the Pacific Ocean three miles up the Lewis and Clark River. The area literally teemed with deer and elk.

The party lodged in Fort Clatsop and killed 20 deer and 100 elk in order to survive the winter and departed in the spring on March 23, 1806.

The Clapsop Indians were peaceable, but demanded much of the party, depleting much of their supply of gifts and trade goods. The fort is now administered by the National Park Service.

Indians came in to the fur trade forts bringing animal pelts. They traded for all manner of beads, steel knives, guns and ammunition. There were all sorts of varieties of goods the posts stocked. Many times the Indians put up their tipis in a circle near the forts, while they conducted trade.

Wagon trains forging westward made stops at trading posts on their route. The immigrants and miners stocked up on goods and supplies and grub at the trading posts.

Fort Union was established along the north bank of the Missouri just above the mouth of the Yellowstone for trade with the

Assiniboine Indians in 1829 by the American Fur Trade Company at the request of the Assiniboine, who desired the trade. The Assiniboine provided protection for the fort. The post became the main fort on the Yellowstone River and has since been reconstructed. It remained active until 1867and was the longest standing post in America.

In the northwest, there were military forts, private fur forts, those owned by large fur companies and there were also alcohol runners, who sold illegal whiskey to the Indians causing alcoholism and bloodshed. The forts were called "Whiskey Forts."

Fort Henry (1822-1828) was named for Andrew Henry. It was located at the junction of the Missouri and the Yellowstone Rivers. Indians destroyed the fort in 1823.

Two major fur trade companies competed for the fur trade industry in the Pacific Northwest: the Hudson's Bay Company and the North West Company. The Hudson's Bay Company was the first fur company established in America creating Fort Vancouver in Oregon Territory.

John McLoughlin erected Fort Vancouver as headquarters for the Hudson's Bay Company and for trade with the Indians in 1824. In addition, several U.S. Army forts and fur forts were raised in Crow Country.

Fort Cass (1832-1835), also known as Tulloch's Fort, named for the founder, Samuel Tulloch of the American Fur Company, was located three miles below the mouth of the Big Horn River on the east bank of the Yellowstone River intended for trade with the Crow Indians; it was surrounded by cottonwood pickets and bastions. The fort was renamed Fort Van Buren, and abandoned in 1835.

The fur trapper Bill Sublette of the American Fur Company opened "Fort Laramie" along the Oregon Trail in 1834. Fort Laramie was a landmark established at the confluence of the Laramie and North Platte Rivers in what is now Wyoming. Trade was initiated between the fur traders and the local Indians. Built of sun-baked adobe bricks, walls contained loopholes for rifle barrels. It became a favorite stopping place for emigrant wagons bound for California.

An old cemetery on the grounds dated back to the fur traders. The fort was converted to a good sized army post with 150 structures. Fort Laramie became a soldier fort, protected settlers from hostile Indians and kept the peace. Fort Laramie Hospital had a 12 bed ward, dispensary, dining room and post surgeon's office. The hospital was the first building constructed of lime grout cement.

In defeating the Sioux twice, General Sully destroyed their encampments, provisions and tons of buffalo meat. Sully had blazed Fort Berthold, Fort Rice and Fort Union through Sioux Country.

In 1865, the Crow assisted the United States protecting the immigrants and miners passing through Sioux country along the Bozeman Trail.

Pierre Choteau and Company operated Fort Clark and Fort Berthold fur trade posts in present day North Dakota on the Missouri upriver from Fort Pierre, which served the Arikara, Hidatsa, Mandan and Sioux Indians. They were an agrarian community planting beans, corn and squash, who lived in earth-lodges, and hunted buffalo.

Fort Pierre was originally a fur trade fort of the American Fur Trade Company on the west bank of the Missouri River, three miles above the mouth of the Bad River since 1832, before Pierre Choteau bought the fort in 1834. The traders bartered with Hunkpapa, Lakota and Yanktonia Sioux Indians. The "wasichus" (palefaces) that the Sioux Natives traded with were largely French and Indian mix bloods. These traders were rowdy, unschooled louts. The Sioux Indians brought buffalo robes for trade and would rather trade than fight.

Fort Jackson, named for Andrew Jackson was built in 1833 as a fur trading post by Francis A. Chardon at the mouth of the Poplar River. The post was 50 feet square. The fort was abandoned in 1834.

Fort Fox and Livingston was a fur trade fort from 1842-1844 built to compete with the American Fur Trade Company. It was located eleven miles below Fort Benton on the east bank near Shonkin Creek. In 1844, the fort moved to Fort Lewis. In 1845, Fort Lewis was purchased by the American Fur Trade Company.

Fort Alexander (1842-1850) was also called Fort Crow by the Blackfoot Indians who opposed its construction. It was established as a non-military fort by fur trader Charles Larpentuer on the left bank of the Yellowstone River opposite the mouth of the Rosebud River.

It was named for Albert Culbertson of the North West Company. It replaced Fort Van Buren and was abandoned in 1850 and moved to Fort Sarpy.

Fort Benton (1846-1881) an initially established fur fort by Alexander Culbertson of the American Fur Trade Company in present day northwestern Montana was an adobe structure of Missouri River mud.

Culbertson's home, barn, blacksmith shop trade quarters and warehouse was surrounded by a 20 foot bastion. In 1865, the fur trade declined and the North West Company sold to the U.S. Army.

Crow Maiden with Doll
(Photograph Courtesy of Azusa Publishing, LLC)

Cantonment Jordan (1859-1860), near De Borgia, Montana and Cantonment Wright (1861-1862), near Milltown, Montana were Winter quarters for John Muller's crew that built the Mullan road from Fort Benton to Walla-Walla, Washington.

In 1860, Fort Dauphin was established as a fur trade post at the mouth of the Milk River by Yuris Dauphin. A French trapper was killed near the fort.

In 1864, Captain James Fisk and 50 Cavalrymen led a wagon train leaving Minnesota early in July of 1864 across Steven's route from Fort Ridgely along the Minnesota River to Fort Rice on the Missouri River in southern North Dakota Territory, while Fort Rice was under construction. Fort Rice was built on the west bank of the Missouri ten miles above the mouth of the Cannonball River.

The immigrant wagon train was en route to the Montana gold fields, when besieged by marauding Sioux Indians. A breastwork of prairie sod was used to build a fortress to defend themselves from the Sioux.

It was named Fort Dilts for Jeffrey Dilts who died attempting to defend them. The siege lasted 14 days until they were rescued and taken to Fort Rice. Eight of the Cavalry were killed and a number of civilians.

In 1864, soldiers built Fort Sully in southern Dakota Territory on the east side of the Missouri River a few miles below Fort Pierre. Fort Sully was a garrison fort that served to quarter U.S. Army personnel.

Fort Fizzle was a temporary fortress built about five miles above the Lolo Canyon in July 25, 1877 by Captain C.C. Rawn who intended to stop the Nez Perce during Joseph's Retreat. The operation failed and was later referred to as "Fort Fizzle."

Fort Hawley, named for A.F. Hawley, was established in 1866 as a trading post constructed for fur trade with the River Crow Indians by Louis Rivet of the North West Company below Fort Benton on the south side of the Missouri twenty miles above the Musselshell.

The fort had begun to deteriorate by 1869 when the Army troops moved in. The fort was abandoned in 1875. In 1908, the Daughters of the American Revolution purchased Fort Benton and restored it to good condition. It remains in place as a museum today.

Fort Campbell (1847-1860) was constructed of adobe brick by the Missouri Fur Company. Alexander Harvey ran the fort. It rivaled Fort Benton, roughly a mile away, for the Indian fur trade.

Fort Campbell competed with the American Fur Company on the Upper Missouri River. In 1860, the Chouteau Company bought Fort Campbell. It was later established as a Jesuit Monastery. The site is located in the Fort Benton Historic District.

Colonel Henry Carrington and hundreds of infantrymen built three forts in Crow and Sioux Indian territory along the Bozeman Trail: Forts C.F. Smith, Kearny, and Reno to defend miners and settlers along the Bozeman trail from Fort Laramie to the mines.

Abraham Lincoln established Montana Territory in 1864.

In 1866, Chief Red Cloud declared war against the U.S. Army because they built soldier forts in the Powder River Valley on the Bozeman Trail, through Sioux hunting grounds, violating the Laramie Treaty.

Fort Ellis was established as a military post in 1867 for the purpose of protecting the miners and settlers in the Galatin Valley of western Montana, Bozeman and neighboring settlements from the marauding Indians and the Sioux Wars 1876-1881.

Colonel John Gibbon used Fort Ellis and Fort Shaw for his operations. He left Fort Ellis to attack Joseph's Nez Perce at Big Hole, Montana. Fort Ellis is now occupied by Montana State University's Fort Ellis Experimental Station three and one half miles east of Bozeman.

Fort Totten was constructed near Devil's Lake in 1867 in northern Dakota Territory, along the Cheyenne River. It was a sub-fort of Tulloch's Fort Cass, designed for trade with the Crow Indians.

Fort Browning Military Post (1868-1873) was built on People's Creek and the milk River two miles southwest of Dodson, Montana. The fort was named for Secretary of State, O.H. Browning. It served as an Indian Agency for the Assiniboine and the Upper Sioux Indians and was abandoned in 1873.

Fort Belknap (1871-1886) was a trading post located near the Milk River in northwestern Montana Territory, named for Robert L. Belknap and later became a station for the Great Northern Railroad.

The purpose of the fort was to serve as the Indian Agency for the Fort Belknap Indian Reservation in eastern Blaine County for the Assiniboine and Sioux Indians and served as a sub-agency for the Crow Indians. Today, the reservation remains in Harlem, Montana.

Fort McKean was built in 1872 on the west bank of the Missouri as a military post in Dakota Territory to secure the Northern Pacific Railroad. The Indians called the locomotive the "Iron Horse."

Fort Janeaux (1873-1883), also referred to as Medicine Lodge, was established by Francis A. Janeaux in partnership with the Leighton Company for a trading post in 1879 on Big Spring Creek. The outpost was 100 x 150 feet stockade with bastions in two of the corners. Francis Janeaux later founded Lewistown, Montana.

Fort Abraham Lincoln was expanded to house six companies of the 7th Cavalry under the command of Lt. Col. George A. Custer in 1873 and was established to guarantee expansion of the American frontier.

By 1874, Fort Abraham Lincoln was the largest and most important post in Dakota Territory that housed 650 cavalrymen and infantrymen.

The Black Hills expeditionary party was launched led by George A. Custer. Gold was discovered on the expedition in the Black Hills. Homesteaders, miners, prospectors, and traders flooded the area. Freight train convoys transported goods into Canada.

On May 17, 1876, the five companies of the 7th Cavalry under George Armstrong Custer rode out from Fort Abraham Lincoln for the Little Bighorn. In 1883, the cavalry was detached to Fort Meade, South Dakota, causing a decline in the use of Fort Abraham Lincoln. It was abandoned in 1891 under the order of Congress.

Fort Custer was established in 1877 by the U.S. Army on Montana's southern border, between the Bighorn and Little Bighorn Rivers, south of what is now Hardin, Montana. The post was named for General George A. Custer. Fort Custer was designed to control the Crow Indians. There was an uprising at the Crow Agency in 1886.

Fort Carroll (1874-1882) and the Diamond R Transportation Company was a private enterprise founded by Matthew Carroll. Goods were shipped from St. Paul, Minnesota by rail on the Northern Pacific Railroad to Bismarck, North Dakota where the rails ended. Goods were shipped from there up the Missouri by steamboat to Fort Carroll. Carroll transported freight and passengers from the docks of the Missouri River overland to the gold fields of Helena.

Fort Macleod was an important Canadian trading post established in 1874 deep in Blackfoot Country for the Blackfoot, Blood and Piegan bands by the Northwest Mounted Police to protect the Canadian sovereignty. Col. James Macleod was the founder.

At the time, whiskey traders were trading "firewater" to the Blackfoot Indians for beaver, buffalo and wolf skins. Forts East End Post, Walsh, Post Qu Appelle, Whoop-up, and Wood Mountain Post also lay over the Canadian border.

Chief Sitting Bull and the Sioux Indians visited Fort Garry during his retreat into Canada in 1877. The Chief's band of 15 lodges camped there on the Red River. The Sioux also rode to Fort Ellis, four days from Fort Garry, where they were fed.

Fort Assiniboine (1878-1911) was established after the Black Hills War with the Sioux to defend against any hostile Nez Perce or Sioux Indians and had 100 buildings. Fort Harrison was a garrison of smaller forts and in 1895 was moved to Fort William Henry Harris.

Fort Yellowstone was constructed by the U.S. Army and was the longest standing post. The fort was established in order to protect the resources at Mammoth Hot Springs, Wyoming from 1888-1918 and was America's first National Park, Yellowstone National Park.

Fort Howes was constructed of stone blocks on a slope above the Howe's ranch south of Ashland, built as a fortress against hostile Cheyenne Indians in 1897. It was also called "Howe's House."

Fort Buford was constructed in northeastern North Dakota near Montana's eastern border, two miles down the Missouri opposite the mouth of the Yellowstone. It was a built on a rocky-river bed.

The fort was designed with stockade and blockhouses for its defense. In 1864, Fort Gilbert was a fur trade fort established on the southern perimeter of the military, Fort Buford on the west bank of the Yellowstone River. The fort was named after Col. Charles Gilbert, who once was a commander at Fort Buford.

Fort Peck was in northern Montana on the fork of the Milk and Missouri Rivers. Fort Shaw lay along the Missouri River in present day northwestern Montana. Fort Keogh was an Indian Agency that sat between the Tongue and the Yellowstone Rivers.

List of Common Trade Goods

Awls, Axes, Beads, Beaver hats, Brass & copper kettles, Bullets and lead, Butcher knives, Buttons, Calico, Candy, Cloth, Coats, Fire steels, Gunflints, Guns, Gunpowder, Hats, Horses, Knives, Lariettes, Oilcloth, Pans, Razors, Saddles, Salt, Scissors, Seashells, Shirts, Sugar, Tea, Thread, Tinkling cones, Tin pots, Tobacco, Pipes, Tomahawks, Trade axes, Trade guns & Wampum.

Chief Red Cloud
(Photograph Courtesy of Azusa Publishing, LLC)

CHAPTER EIGHT
BLUE COATS

Born in Ohio, George Crook, a graduate from West Point in 1852, put down the Paiute War in 1860 and enrolled in the Civil War from 1861 to 1865. At the war's end, Crook learned first-hand about the Indians. Dealing with them in California and Oregon, he observed how treaties were broken and was sympathetic to their cause.

General Crook assumed command of the Department of the Columbia over Indian uprisings on Jordan Creek, Oregon, the Owyhee River, the Malheur Lake area, and along Dunder and Blitzen Creek in 1866. Skirmishes were fought on the John Day, Lake Albert, and Harney Lake areas until 1867, as Red Cloud's War was fought in the Powder River Valley and along the Yellowstone.

In the field, Crook wore uniforms made to order. He wore a pith helmet or straw hat for headgear. A cotton jacket was worn over a civilian shirt, tucked into breeches with riding boots usually knee-high. He also wore buckskin jackets, trousers and leggings.

In the autumn of 1866, Chief Red Cloud returned to the Powder River country and found that the "wasichus" (white man) had moved 200 miles into Sioux territory from Fort Laramie.

Red Cloud knew the Army had broken the provisions of the Laramie Treaty and summoned the scattered bands of Arapahoe, Cheyenne and Sioux to assemble for council, after their bison hunts.

When their allies arrived, they sat in council and spoke of the white man's advance. After Red Cloud declared war in 1866, the Arapahoe, Cheyenne and Sioux attacked the soldiers at Fort Phil Kearny and made numerous raids on the soldier fort.

Colonel Carrington chose the Sioux's favorite hunting grounds to build Fort Phil Kearny, asking for trouble. Soldiers felled trees to build the stockade fort. He used the fort as his headquarters. Suddenly, a crew of Carrington's woodcutters that was working northwest of the Fort Phil Kearny was attacked by Chief Crazy Horse and a Sioux Indian war party. Captain Fetterman led a small band of Cavalry that came to their rescue, but rode into a Sioux ambush that left two soldiers dead and some wounded.

U.S. Army Captain Fetterman led 80 Cavalrymen and streaked out of Fort Phil Kearney in pursuit of Crazy Horse's war party on December 21, 1866. The Chief and nine warriors rode ahead of them as decoys down to the valley below, where thousands of braves lay in ambush. All 81 cavalrymen were massacred. As help arrived, they saw Sioux warriors ride off in the distance.

General Sully twice defeated the Sioux, destroyed villages, supplies and tons of buffalo meat. He had blazed Fort Berthold, Fort Union, and Fort Rice through Sioux territory and manned all three army posts with soldiers in Sioux country along the Bozeman Trail.

The forts were meant to protect immigrants and miners passing through, aided in their protection by Crow Indian Army scouts in 1865. Fort Rice was located on the west bank of the Missouri ten miles above the mouth of the Cannonball River.

George Armstrong Custer earned recognition at West Point as a young illustrious officer, who gained rank in the Union Army during the Civil War. Custer was transferred out West to lead the 7th U.S. Cavalry in 1867 and was assigned to command Fort Lincoln. Lt. Colonel George Custer received a court martial in 1867 for the

George "Longhair" Custer
(Photograph Courtesy of Azusa Publishing, LLC)

mistreatment of his men and abandoning his post, yet had earlier ordered deserters shot in cold blood. He was found guilty and relieved of duty for a year. In 1868 he was restored to his command.

During a snow storm, Custer followed Cheyenne tracks and attacked the Cheyenne at dawn. The chief and his wife rode out to meet Custer under a white flag, but they were shot down by the cowardly Custer. He was ordered to bring the Cheyenne and Sioux onto the reservations, but ignored the orders and massacred them at the Battle of Washita, killing and scalping Chief Black Kettle.

Among the captured, Custer saw a beautiful Cheyenne woman and took her as his mistress. He and his wife, Libbie had no children, but he sired a bastard child with his Cheyenne lover, Monahseta.

Smohalla, a Nez Perce prophet, initiated the Dreamer's Religion and proclaimed that Indians would rise up from the dead and drive the white-eyes from the land in 1872. Wavoca, a Paiute holy man in Nevada, called Jack Wilson, had a vision of immortal warriors in Ghost shirts dancing in a circle, invincible to paleface bullets and started the "Ghost Shirt Religion." Frenzy spread across the Plains, reaching the Crow; hundreds of Indians rallied to fight the white man.

In 1872, a Crow Indian Agent deputized two white men and arrested two Bannock Indians accused of stealing Crow horses. One Bannock ran and was shot dead. A Crow chief, named "Little Iron," killed a Flathead. Crow companions of the Flathead who died vowed to kill two of Little Iron's Bannock friends. The chief threatened to kill the Crow Agent, but he opened his shops and gave everyone presents, as a reprieve for sparing his life. The Crow land size was again reduced in 1872. The Agency moved to Absarokee, Montana.

Plenty Coups "Chief Crow Scout"
(Courtesy of Nez Perce.com)

Crook led the campaign against the Apache in the southwest. The Lt. Colonel brought Cochise to the peace table in 1872 and was promoted to Brigadier General on October 29. 1873.

In 1874, Lt. Col. Custer violated the 1868 Laramie Treaty and led an expedition of his 7th Cavalry, geologists, miners, newspaper men, 100 wagons and a large party of civilians to explore the Black Hills. They discovered gold and rich farmable land, starting a huge gold rush. Miners clambered all over Sioux land. The government continued to buy the land, but the Sioux refused to sell them the Black Hills.

In 1875, Custer's orders were to march up river from Fort Lincoln. Crook's Column would sweep northward from Fort Fetterman into the Powder River region. Fort Fetterman was a military outpost on the Platte River in southeastern Wyoming.

Crook was transferred to take command of the Department of the Platte in Omaha and the Bighorn-Yellowstone Expedition in 1875, a seasoned Indian fighter; Indians called him, "Grey Fox."

Sheridan began a winter campaign against the Sioux. That winter, Crook defeated Chief Dull Knife and his band of Cheyenne. Terry gave Reno written orders to scout the Tongue River area for Indians and pushed on to the Powder River country. Gibbon's forces would rendezvous with Custer's column in May, but operations stalled in blizzard conditions the winter of 75-76.

The Sioux were given the ultimatum to be on reservations by January 31, 1876, or be declared hostiles, but they did not receive word and continued to fight. The U.S. Army pushed on to defeat the Sioux and Cheyenne Indian hostiles.

CHAPTER NINE
CROW INDIAN SCOUTS

Fur traders, frontiersmen, mountain men and trappers who knew the territory and spoke Indian dialects were hired as Army scouts. Such were Buffalo Bill, Jim Bridger and Kit Carson.

When the Sioux and Cheyenne went to war, they urged the Crow Indians to join them against the palefaces. Instead, the Crow did the opposite and took up arms against them.

Governor Potts of Montana Territory wrote a letter to the United States government urging them to hire Crow Indian warriors as army scouts. The army began to hire them. A separate branch called the "U.S. Army Scouts" was created. Indians enlisted, were given social acceptance, and played a key-roll in the Indian Wars.

In 1876, Fort Boise was an outpost to dispatch militia to protect settlers during the Indian Wars and a post to house George Crook's militia. He set up a base camp ready to rout any hostiles.

In June of 1876, General Crook received a message from Sioux Chief Crazy Horse. The message was brief and to the point. It said every soldier that crossed was the north of the Tongue River would die.

Crow Scouts were first used by the U.S. Army in 1876, during the Great Sioux War. Peaceable Crow braves were enlisted to help track enemy Indian hostiles. Colonel Gibbon met with War Chief Medicine Crow on the Yellowstone and told the Crows that their Sioux enemy had been killing the Crow people and white man too long and he was going to punish them and advised them it was time to make war against the Sioux.

113

He said it was time to stop their war parties and avenge their fallen comrades. Thirty Crow Indian braves joined Gibbon as scouts.

The Plains Crow were excellent trackers. Tracks of different tribes varied and could be identified by them. Footprints of the Arapahoe, Blackfeet, Cheyenne and Sioux, for instance, were different shapes and the tracker knew the identities.

They could detect a broken twig, bent blade of grass, broken branch or an impression in the earth was quickly detected. The time that the markings were made was known and approximately how far ahead the enemy was. In the same way, the Indians tracked animals to hunt game.

The "Wolves" of the Crow Indian militant society joined the U.S. Army as scouts for vengeance against their bitter enemies, the Sioux. A Mountain Crow, Plenty Coups was Chief of Scouts over 170 Crow Wolves.

They wore wolf skins for camouflage. A wolf howl from a Crow scout alerted the pack. Plenty Coups advised Wolves to cooperate with the army against the Sioux because, "When the war is over, the soldier-chiefs will not forget that the Crows came to their aid."

As scouts, the Crow were able to punish enemy tribes that they had fought, in particular the Sioux. The Sioux were a fierce tribe fighting against the United States.

In Montana the Crow contested the hunting grounds with the Teton Sioux. Their hatred for the Sioux was an additional reason they joined up to be U.S. Army scouts; they hoped to gain back their hunting grounds.

Custer's Crow Scout, Curly
(Photograph Courtesy of Azusa Publishing, LLC)

Crow Scout "White Man Runs Him"
(Photograph Courtesy of Azusa Publishing, LLC)

Crow Army Scout "Goes Ahead"
(Photograph Courtesy of Azusa Publishing, LLC)

Custer's Scouts at Battlefield
(Photograph Courtesy of Azusa Publishing, LLC)

"Red Wing," Mountain Crow Scout for Custer
(Photograph Courtesy of Azusa Publishing, LLC)

The Crow Indians provided the very best scouts for the U.S. Army and made loyal guides and scouts, many were Mountain Crows. The U.S. Army provided them with guns and ammunition, horses and goods.

Curley was one such scout. He was born in 1856 and married Bird Woman. Goes Ahead had many names, including Rides Alone, and Child-of-the-Stars. He too became a scout. Goes Ahead was married to Pretty Shield, a famous medicine woman and lived on the reserve. He died in 1919; she was interred next to him. Crow women often became medicine women.

Curley divorced Bird Woman and married Takes-a-Shield. They had a daughter, Bird-of-Another-Year. He served as Crow Police and died May 21, 1923, at the Crow Agency. All of the above were buried at the Little Bighorn National Cemetery.

Hairy Moccasin was another scout. White-Man-Runs-Him, a Mountain Crow was born into the Big Lodge Clan, and became a scout. He died in 1929. Pretty Eagle was a Mountain Crow scout.

Chief Washakie was the famous tribal chief of the Green and Wind River Goshute Shoshoni Indians, in Wyoming Territory. Sacajawea visited her people about the same time. Washakie led 300 Shoshoni warriors to the 1837 Rendezvous.

Washakie grew to be a man and as a warrior rode among Blackfeet, Crow and Sioux scaring their horses with his buffalo skin rattle that sounded like a rattlesnake; horses reared, or bolted, and threw their riders. He was a stately six foot chief. Washakie signed treaties at Forts Laramie and Bridger. His daughter married Jim Bridger.

Washakie's Shoshoni Village
(Photograph Courtesy of the Smithsonian Institute)

A Blackfoot raiding war party took horses from the Shoshoni. Washakie tracked them north for 600 miles, retrieved the horses, and took enemy scalps.

Ten years previous, he led a war party against the Crow Indians and fought for several days until the fighting stopped. Washakie and Crow Chief, Big Robber, agreed to fight a duel over the hunting grounds in Wind River Valley. Washakie shot and killed him.

Washakie cut out Big Robber's heart and paraded back and forth with the organ on the point of his lance to show respect for the courage of Big Robber. The Crow watched in awe. He hoisted the lance until after the Shoshoni had held their victory dance. The Crow tribe never attacked the Eastern Shoshoni again; the site of the duel was called Crow-heart Butte for the famous battle. A Wyoming historical marker was erected on the butte.

Washakie was peaceable to the fur trapper, pioneer, soldier and friend to Kit Carson. He received a silver saddle from Ulysses Grant and also a peace medal from President Johnson in 1866. On June 14, 1876, Crook was joined by Chiefs Good Heart, Medicine Crow, Old Crow and 176 Crow scouts. Washakie and 86 Shoshoni warriors arrived to fight the warring Sioux, who had killed his son. They rode in eloquently and joined the ranks.

After a 60 mile ride from Wind River, the Shoshoni wished to do a war dance. Warriors danced through the night, clad in breech-cloths, moccasins and war paint, wearing bonnets or just feathers. They danced and chanted through the night to the beat of tom-toms. The soldiers in the camp were awake most of the night listening

Shoshoni Chief Washakie
(Photograph Courtesy of Azusa Publishing, LLC)

to the loud war-whoops that filled the air. Soldiers gathered to watch them dancing. The Indians danced into the wee hours of the morning.

Early the following day, General Crook broke camp and crossed the Tongue River. He turned northwest into Sioux territory. The Indian scouts rode out ahead of the troops and returned to report that they had seen a band of Sioux hunting buffalo. In addition, they discovered the tracks indicating the movement of many Sioux Indians. Finding an Indian trail, Crook deployed Reynolds and six men to scout for the village. He marched through bitter snow and cold surprising the Cheyenne and Sioux and seized the village. Reynolds failed to destroy the lodges and returned to the fort.

Crook's troops bivouacked at the headwaters of Rosebud Creek. At dawn, they marched downstream. Crook commanded a halt around 8:00 a.m. and grazed their horses, his infantry caught up. They advanced to a hilly arena. Hills gave way to higher elevations. The Crow grew uneasy. They were unprepared for a sudden Sioux attack. Medicine Crow and Washakie sent out look-outs onto lofty ridges north of their position. Others searched for fresh tracks.

Suddenly, a wounded warrior rode in at a full gallop, shouting, "Sioux, Sioux, many Sioux." Shots were fired as Crook's scouts counter attacked 500 yards ahead. They attacked from the north and west issuing war whoops as the advance party held the Sioux back.

In March of 1876, General Crook moved his troops north from Fort Fetterman, Wyoming through the Powder River Valley to spearhead the attack against the Sioux and strike a decisive blow. Crook moved his supplies by pack-trains and Indian scouts to track the hostiles. Crook was known as the Army's greatest Indian fighter.

His Indian scouts called him "Three Stars," the number of stars on his uniform. He treated them humanely. He would negotiate rather than fight. Sioux Indian hunters returned to their village, having seen Crook's column camped in the Valley of the Little Bighorn on the Great Medicine Dance Creek.

Medicine Crow served as Chief scout leading 176 Crow scouts under Brigadier General Crook, in the Battle of Rosebud one week before the Battle of the Little Bighorn. He was described as wearing a full feathered war

bonnet adorned with buffalo horns and otter fur strips. Chief Plenty Coups also scouted for General Crook.

On June 17th, Brigadier General Crook attacked the Sioux near the headwaters of the Rosebud. Crook's "long-knives" fought the hostiles and were pushed back by Chief Crazy Horse's Cheyenne and Sioux Indian warriors at the Battle of Rosebud River. The next day Crook retreated to the south. When he withdrew, 7,000 Sioux moved their village to the east bank of the Little Bighorn River, who wanted to hunt buffalo. About 2,000 of them were warriors.

Chief Crazy Horse held his massive army back in reserve. It was estimated that there were 2,500 Arapahoe, Cheyenne, and Sioux all hidden in the hills. Perhaps 1,500 were in the initial charge.

Crook backed up his Indian scouts and deployed more in the valley. Washakie was everywhere. He urged his sub-chiefs into battle and spoke to Crook as he rode alongside him, using sign language to discuss the battle. He helped rescue an injured officer. Washakie was naked to the waist, sat on his war pony and wore deerskin britches and and moccasins and a long war bonnet that hung down to the ground.

125

The Crow-Shoshoni scout team regrouped and met the second Sioux assault. Some of the scouts dismounted and fought from the ground. Other scouts rode bravely among the Sioux, firing at close range. A blue-grey din of acrid smoke hung in the air. The bodies of fallen Indians and horses littered the field in the wild roses. Scouts fought far ahead, yet held on. The advance guard of Crow and Shoshoni scouts had saved Crook's column from certain death.

General Crook did not know the extent of Crazy Horse's army and pressed farther northward into hostile territory. He disregarded Washakie's warning that a huge Sioux camp lay ahead and ordered them to attack.

Crook divided his forces and sent a unit ahead under Captain Mills to spearhead their attack, but made an error in judgment by dividing his ranks. Crook ordered Mills back. It was a stroke of luck because, when Captain Mills wheeled his company around, he confronted the warring Sioux that were preparing to attack General Crook's contingent from the north.

Mills quick thinking sandwiched the Sioux between his forces and Crook's army. The Sioux fled the scene by riding around Crook's line and out of sight. General Crook chose to retreat during the night. He led his army back to the fort and retired because of extreme blizzard conditions. Crook claimed victory despite his retreat from battle. Twenty eight men died and 56 were wounded. Only 13 Sioux were killed.

The Sioux did the Sun Dance in early June. Sitting Bull was upset that the white man wanted Sioux land and would not leave. He danced the Sun Dance and mutilated himself, cutting strips of skin.

Captain Fredrick Benteen
(Photograph Courtesy of Azusa Publishing, LLC)

from his forearm. He fasted, prayed taking no food or water. Sitting Bull danced and passed out from exhaustion; when he came to, the Chief had a vision.

In his dream, The Medicine Chief saw long knives descending on them like grasshoppers. The Blue coats fell down in defeat and the Sioux Nation was the victor!

Chief Sitting Bull was a great medicine man and war chief. He was probably the most famous American Indian in our history. From his vision, he predicted the Sioux would deliver a great blow to the U.S. Army. Sitting Bull had much power over thousands of Indians at this time and summoned bands of Arapahoe, Cheyenne, and Sioux to congregate on the Little Bighorn amassing the largest army of Indians ever assembled on the Columbia Plateau.

Two thousand Arapahoe, Cheyenne and Sioux warriors under Chiefs Sitting Bull, Crazy Horse, Gall, Red Cloud, and Spotted Tail assembled on the Rosebud to meet the army's attack.

Mountain Crow warriors, Curley, Goes Ahead, Hairy Moccasin and White-Man-Runs-Him all came from the Crow Agency in Montana and enlisted as U.S. Army scouts on April 10, 1876 to fight the Sioux under Lt. Charles Varnum and George Custer.

The morning of June 22, 1876, the 7th Cavalry was at the mouth of the Rosebud, the soldiers prepared for the march. Terry assigned six Crow scouts to complement the "Ree scouts." Terry's plan was for Custer to advance up the Rosebud to the headwaters and to seek out the Sioux hostiles; he was to make his own decisions and if their trail turned up, go down the Bighorn River to head them off.

War Chief Sitting Bull
(Photograph Courtesy of Azusa Publishing, LLC)

Custer planned to defeat them with 500 men. Terry told Custer where to locate the Sioux. Custer suspected they were on the Rosebud, unsure of their numbers.

The main column advanced. Terry and his officers boarded the steamboat to meet Gibbon. Generals Terry, Custer and Gibbon met with Major Brisbin of the Second Cavalry met on the steamboat, Far West, and discussed the Sioux's movements for over two hours and estimated that they had about 400 lodges with 800 warriors.

The U.S. 7th Cavalry treated the situation as if the Indians were already beaten and soldiers jested about their triumphs early. Little did they know what lay ahead.

The morning of June 23, 1876, the 7th moved out and the Crow and Ree scouts rode out ahead of the company and along the flanks. Varnum scouted up ahead; a Crow scout found an enemy camp at the fork of Davis and Rosebud Creeks. Boyer found travois trails in the sand leading across the divide.

Brisbin's Cavalry moved up the Yellowstone to the mouth of the Little Bighorn and on to the confluence. Benteen and Custer agreed that a frontal attack could let the Sioux escape across the Yellowstone.

They were to join on June 26. They were to engage the hostiles, if any. Terry spearheaded the search for the Sioux in Powder River Valley and the Tongue River before deciding they were camped on the Rosebud. Custer, Reno, and Benteen served under Terry.

Custer's Crow scouts failed to see any Dakota Indians on their journey, but unseen Sioux scouts had observed them. They reported to their chiefs what they saw. Custer's scouts picked up the

Sioux's tracks, but never saw the enemy until they reached their village. Custer's 7th Cavalry moved in a long line from the Yellowstone toward the Little Bighorn. Sioux Indian scouts shadowed the column, unseen by the U.S. Army soldiers as they penetrated Sioux country.

The Crow spoke in the universal sign language of the American Indians. This way, they could converse with the soldiers, officers and the other scouts. Custer used sign with his Crow scouts.

Varnum and his Crow and Ree scouts reached the Crow's Nest, a natural outcropping of rock overlooking the Little Bighorn Valley. They rode up to observe the valley below.

The 7th Cavalry arrived at the Crow's Nest and Custer rode to the top. Boyer and Hairy Moccasin gave Custer the size and position of the Sioux Indians below in the valley. The Crow scouts told him it was the largest concentration of Indians that they had ever seen.

Custer planned to cross the divide before daylight and conceal the regiment before attacking the next day on June 26, but they got a late start. They could hear war-whoops coming from the Sioux village.

When George Custer and the 7th U.S. Army Cavalry left Yellowstone in 1876, the unit had 50 non-military personnel. Lt. Charles Varner was Chief of scouts over six Crow Indian scouts, "Curley," "Goes Ahead," "Hairy Moccasin," "Half-Yellow-Face," "White Swan" and "White-Man-Runs-Him," four Dakota scouts and 39 Arikara scouts. Two Crow scouts, Half-Yellow-Face and White Swan were assigned to Reno. He had 36 civilians in his command.

The Indians referred to Custer as the "Son of the Morning Star," indicating the stars on his uniform. Bloody Knife, Strikes Two and Young Hawk were Ree Indian Scouts that served under Custer. Bloody Knife was his favorite. Two civilian scouts, Mitch Boyer, a half-breed, and Reynolds were guides. Mark Kellogg was a reporter and two were interpreters. Six men were packers.

Crow scouts, Curley, Goes Ahead, Hairy Moccasin and White-Man-Runs-Him all advised Custer to wait for reinforcements, because of the Sioux's large numbers, but Custer would not listen to his scouts, eager to massacre the Sioux. Wearing a buckskin fringed suit, Custer rode among his troops. While Arikara couriers sighted the village and horse herd, Gerard and Bloody Knife rode out to take a look. Bloody Knife predicted a three day fight, but Custer mused that they would whip them in a day.

The village was hard to see even with spyglasses, but the Crow were sure that the enemy had already seen the smoke from their camp fires. Terry was to accompany Gibbon up the Yellowstone to the mouth of the Bighorn River.

The two commands would reconnoiter on June 26th. The next day Terry met with Custer in his tent to give him written orders from Gibbon. Custer was to use his own judgment in attacking the Sioux. They discussed plans for the next day sitting around the campfire. Custer had orders to deploy and seek out the Rosebud Sioux and contain them. The 7th Cavalry maneuvered into a column for a review by Terry and Gibbon. The cadre believed with the regiment of men, artillery, 175 mules and 647 civilians they could defeat them.

Captain Tom Custer, Brother of George "Long Hair"
(Photograph Courtesy of Azusa Publishing, LLC)

The 7th Cavalry had ridden all night in order to reach the Sioux Indian Village in Dakota Territory. The 7th pony soldier was issued a horse, bridle and a McClellan saddle, blanket and haversack, navy blue blouses, light blue kersey trousers, belts, boots, socks, neckerchiefs, gloves, jackets, caps or grey slouch hats.

When Custer's columns arrived at Reno Creek, he divided his five companies into three groups. Reno was assigned two companies, Benteen was assigned one company and Custer had two. They were equipped with 1873 Springfield rifles in slings and 1872 .45 caliber Colt revolvers, ammo, knives, bayonets and sabers. Seasoned veterans, the life of a soldier was hard; they spent hours in the saddle, lacked sleep, exposed to the sun, wind and rain. Winters were grueling, subject to the snow and cold.

Custer's Crow scouts at the Little Bighorn felt that they were about to die in combat with the powerful Sioux, so they stripped down from their blue uniforms to their native garb of loin cloths and moccasins, discarding their old army uniforms. They prepared to die and knew their fate.

When questioned by Custer, they told him they wished to die in their Indian habit.   Hearing this, the general lost his temper and dismissed them as they approached the Sioux village. Custer ordered Boyer and the four Crow scouts to the rear.

Custer had discharged his scouts, but Curley refused to leave. Mitch Boyer insisted that he be dismissed and told the young scout, "We have no chance at all." and instructed him to relay the message to General Terry, that "all were killed."   Other Indian scouts scattered.

In Custer's eyes, Reno had been sent on a suicide mission. The scouts observed that Major Reno's troops had engaged the Sioux in combat. Most of the scouts joined Captain Reno.

The 7th Cavalry was eager to assault the Indians and defeat the adversary. They did not know the size of the village or that they rode into an ambush by thousands of Arapahoe, Cheyenne and Sioux Indian warriors. Sioux scouts detected Custer's column and observed their every move.

On June 25, 1876, Major Reno divided ranks: Captain Benteen rode southwest to Glen Creek and along the east side of the river staying close. Seeing no Indians, he closed up with Reno.

Custer rode onto Montana Hill and observed the Sioux to be running away. Chief Crazy Horse's favorite maneuver in battle was a running decoy stunt, where the warriors pretended to fear the army and ride away from the soldiers in haste. If the soldiers followed, the decoys led them directly into an ambush.

Custer and Reno attacked from both ends of the Rosebud Sioux village. Sitting Bull's adopted brother, Gall, led the attack. The heat was a stifling 100 degrees, as Custer's 7th charged the village.

George Armstrong Custer led the two companies of his 7th Cavalry in hot pursuit of the Sioux Indians along the Little Bighorn River, as the bugler blew charge, with the American flag waving.

As Reno attacked at the other end of the village, Chief Gall routed Reno's troops and met Custer's forces head on with hundreds of Sioux warriors for a decisive frontal attack.

Hunkpapa Sioux Indian Chief Rain-in-the-Face painted half his face red and the other half black to represent the sun. One day he had fought all day in the rain. His war-paint ran down in streaks and he earned the name, Rain-in-the-Face.

Rain-in-the-Face had been humiliated being arrested by Captain Tom Custer (Little Hair), brother of Lt. Colonel George Armstrong Custer and swore that someday he would cut out his heart.

Rain-in-the-Face made good his vow at Greasy Grass. He sang the war-song, smelled the blue grey acrid smoke of battle, and his anger rose. The chief ran in and grasped the bluecoats' flag, clubbed the soldier with his tomahawk and ran back to his ranks with the flag.

He mounted his horse, caught sight of "Little Hair" and spurred his steed toward him, but his pony was shot out from under him. He caught and mounted another horse. The chief killed a bluecoat with his tomahawk as he closed in on Custer.

Rain-in-the-Face saw fear in his enemy's eyes and shot him with his revolver. He rode off, gratified, but sick of war. Chief Rain-in-the-Face later denied any mutilation of Tom Custer.

Custer was vastly outnumbered. Major Reno was engaged in heavy combat with the Sioux; then he got into trouble. Benteen rallied and came to Reno's rescue. Reno's army, having received reinforcements, had the strength needed to fight on.

Goes Ahead, Hairy Moccasin and White-Man-Runs-Him joined Reno fighting the Sioux briefly atop a ridge as the battle abruptly ended. Reno retreated and escaped with heavy losses. Colonel Gibbon and his troops came to Major Reno's rescue on June 26th. The Crow Scouts were later assigned to Colonel Gibbon's outfit.

136

Chief Rain-in-the-Face
(Photograph Courtesy of Azusa Publishing, LLC)

Custer's battalion fought for their lives surrounded by Indians; two hundred ten men were massacred in the Battle of the Little Bighorn. Civilian scouts, Charley Reynolds, Isaiah Dorman, Mitch Boyer, Ree scouts, Bloody Knife and Bob-Tail-Bull were killed in action. Goose, White Swan and, Herendeen were wounded.

George Armstrong Custer died June 25, 1876, what is now known as "Custer's Last Stand." He made a fatal mistake dividing his five companies at the Little Bighorn that cost him the lives of his brother, Tom, his cousin, Boston, his nephew, Autie Reed, his company and his own life: 210 soldiers in all.

Reportedly, Curley observed the battle gazing through spy glasses from a ridge one-half mile away. He had eluded the Sioux by crawling through the coulees, before he reached a dead Sioux warrior.

Taking his horse and blanket, Curley rode day and night for 48 hours straight, until he reached the steamboat Far West. Curley used Indian sign language to convey the fate of the 7th Cavalry, but the full extent of the massacre was not realized then.

The sun went down. The Sioux did a victory dance. The Crow scouts disbanded. Goes Ahead, Hairy Moccasin, and White-Man-Runs-Him rode to the Bighorn River, camped the night and the next day, Crow scouts from Bradley's command crossed the river with them and they rode to the Crow Camp, two sleeps distant.

After Sitting Bull defeated Custer and the 7th Cavalry, he was wanted by the U.S. Army to be hunted down and killed in America, his Sioux people unsafe. Many Sioux found refuge on reservations. The Army pursued as the Sioux fled into Canada; many yielded to Miles, whom the Indians called, "Bear Coat." They respected him.

Mackenzie's troops sacked and burned the Cheyenne camp of Chiefs Dull Knife and Little Wolf. The army occupied the Dakota's hunting grounds, leaving little to eat. Indians had to contend with the cold as temperatures plummeted.

The military could converge on them camp at any time, annihilate them, burn their teepees and shoot their horses. Sitting Bull and his band endured the cold, harsh winter of 1876-1877, not wanting to give up Sioux lands in unconditional surrender forcing them onto reservations. Most Sioux were contained at the Agencies.

Sitting Bull's people were starving, their horses gaunt, yet he would not give in to their demands and knew they could find refuge in the White Mother's country. The chief made the long trek from Montana into Grandmother's country (Canada) with 1,000 Sioux.

The Nez Perce War escalated on June 17, 1877. Major Green's Cavalry and 20 Bannock scouts, led by Buffalo Horn, who had served as scout for General Crook in the Sioux War, rode out of Fort Boise to join Howard's 7th Cavalry against the Nez Perce.

In 1877, during the Nez Perce War, under Chief Joseph, Chiefs Looking Glass, Too-hul-hut-sote, and White Bird wanted to join the Crow Indians in "buffalo country."

The Crow were their enemies and Joseph did not want to leave "the land of their fathers." Joseph, a born leader led his whole village, with an estimated 750 tribes-people and some 400 mounted warriors into battle. The Nez Perce rode splendid Appaloosa horses and herded over 2,000 head of horses and pack mules, as they retreated toward Canada. Horses pulled travois carrying loads of goods, hides, and infants.

139

Looking Glass had ridden ahead to parley with the Crow Indians and ask for refuge, but they chose neutrality. Scouts told Joseph Sturgis was ahead and the prairie was burning. The Nez Perce rode toward Canada; Joseph sent warriors toward Hart Mountain. They dragged brush bundles behind their horses and hid their tracks.

Bear Coat was camped on the Tongue River under pressure to bring in Sitting Bull. Head scout, Medicine Crow joined the U.S. Army under Bear Coat, and led the Crow scouts that pursued Chief Sitting Bull and his band as he fled into Canada, in May of 1877.

Sitting Bull escaped to Canada about the time Crazy Horse surrendered at Fort Robinson and Miles defeated a small band of Yankton Sioux, ending the "Great Sioux War."

Crow warriors chased the Nez Perce clear across their territory in a running battle that stretched over 150 miles. The Nez Perce lost 900 spent horses.

Crows fought them to within 40 miles of the Musselshell River before retreating. By 1877, the Crow fought the Arapaho, Cheyenne, and Sioux north as far as Canada.

In 1877, Chief Medicine Crow rode under Miles as Chief Army scout and pursued Joseph in his retreat to the Bear Paw Mountains during the Nez Perce War to defeat the Nez Perce.

On May 6, 1877, after continuous pressure from the U.S. military and with the lack of buffalo for subsistence, Chief Crazy Horse and his band of 1,000 Sioux people surrendered at Fort Robinson, Nebraska. Chief Crazy Horse had fought brilliantly against the U.S. Army trying to save his land, but the odds were against him and time ran out.

Nez Perce Chief Joseph
(Photograph Courtesy of Azusa Publishing, LLC)

Buffalo Horn had served as Bannock scout for General George Custer in the Sioux War and had also completed a dangerous mission for Nelson A. Miles along the Yellowstone River, with a Crow scout, Le Forge and Buffalo Bill Cody.

In 1878, an incident occurred between Bannock Indians and some farmers on the Camas Prairie. Chief Buffalo Horn led the Bannock Indians into war.

The Nez Perce and the Bannock Indians were enemies. The Bannock marauders rode across Idaho and Oregon killing settlers and stealing their livestock. Chief Buffalo Horn was killed in a running battle with the Silver City Volunteers.

Colonel Nelson A. Miles engaged the renegade Bannock, in 1878. In an early morning raid, Miles, with 75 Cavalry plus Crow Indian scouts in a surprise attack on the hostiles, killed eleven ending the Bannock War.

In 1880, the Piegan held a Sun Dance. Chiefs Bad Head, Medicine Calf, and White Calf sat in council with Crow Chiefs Pregnant Woman and Was Kicked and smoked the peace pipe, who accepted the gesture. The Assiniboine and Gros Ventre joined the celebration in peace.

The Sun Dance was thought to be a form of torture and viewed as evil by the settlers. In 1880, the Sun Dance was banned in America and again from 1904-1935. A milder form of the Sun Dance is practiced today.

In 1880, General Crook was promoted to Major General by President Cleveland and placed over the whole Western theater. Twelve American Indian Medal of Honor winners were decorated.

Sitting Bull and the Hunkpapa band made the long trek back from Canada in 1881. That summer, Sitting Bull's party arrived at Fort Buford.

On July 19, 1881, Sitting Bull and nine hundred eighty six Hunkpapa surrendered at Fort Buford, North Dakota. Sitting Bull surrendered his Winchester carbine to authorities and was sent to Fort Randall and imprisoned for his war crimes, with no promised pardon.

White Calf, Peigan hunters and the Crows hunted buffalo where they could find herds. Scouts rode ahead to locate them. By 1881, the bison had gone from Yellowstone and they faced starvation.

The band returned to Canada in the spring of 1882, White Calf's band reached the reserve in Alberta. He had no choice but to live on rations in the absence of buffalo; they ate beef and flour. They added to their diet eating a deer or prairie chicken they shot on the Belly River, which kept them alive. White Calf prevented reckless braves from going on the warpath and honored the treaties that he had made with the Crow, Gros Ventre and Assiniboine.

Crow scouts, who served in the U.S. Army and fought in the Indian Wars, were promised tracts of land in the Bighorn Mountains and on the Bighorn River Valley, in their sacred lands.

In 1882, Crook returned to Arizona and forced Geronimo to the peace talks, but he vanished in the hills. Colonel Nelson A. Miles replaced Crook, and ended the Apache Wars exiling Geronimo's band and Apache scouts to Florida. Crook never forgave Miles.

In 1890, the American Indian Scout branch of the Army's insignia was crossed arrows; the same insignia was adopted by the Navy Seals in 1984 for the Special Forces' patch.

Colonel Nelson A. Miles was promoted to the position of general, as Commander-in Chief of the U.S. Army, in 1895.

Five Indians in the 20th Century received the Medal of Honor for heroism beyond the call of duty; some made the ultimate sacrifice for their country.

The fact that the Crow were friendly to the palefaces and volunteered to scout for the U.S. Army did not set well with other Indian tribes. They felt that they had gone over to the enemy and were traitors. The Crows informed on other tribes, like the Sioux. Some of these tribes despised the Crow for their actions.

George Armstrong Custer was guilty of massacring Cheyenne and Sioux Indian villages, yet the Crow served as Indian scouts under him. Some of these tribes despised the Crow for their actions.

Joe Medicine Crow was born October 27, 1913. He was the grandson of Crow Indian Chiefs, Medicine Crow and Yellowtail, the last war chief of the Crow Nation. He sat in the sweat lodge and listened to the warrior tales told by his elders. Joe entered the service as an Army scout for the 103rd Infantry Division during World War II.

In combat Medicine Crow wore his war paint under his uniform and his sacred feather beneath his helmet. In the tradition of a Crow warrior, he touched a German enemy and disarmed him, counted his first and second coups. Joe led a night raid, stole German horses and sang a Crow Indian war song of honor, as he rode away.

Joseph Medicine Crow was the recipient of the Bronze Star Medal, the Legion of Honneur, and Presidential Medal of Freedom. Joseph Medicine Crow is a member of the Crow Nation, patriot, brave warrior and the last Chief of the Crow Nation.

Joseph Medicine Crow was a historian and author of Native American history. The Crow Indians were a proud race and served in the Army as strong warriors.

Native American Army Scouts existed until 1947, when the last one retired. Although the American Indian Army Scouts were disbanded in 1947, their contribution of loyalty and bravery shown in the time of war defines the determination and heroism that they exhibited like the courage of their ancestors in battle in days of old.

Joseph Medicine Crow was just one of thousands of American Indians, who fought for the nobel cause in W.W.II. The American Indians serving in the Armed Forces exhibited the kind of bravery that their ancestors did on the battlefield years before.

Our thanks go out to those Native American men and women, who fought for our country back then.

Navajo Code Talkers served in W.W.II. The Navajo Code Talkers accomplished their mission. The Japanese military could not break the secret code of the American Indian's dialect.

Code talkers from other tribes served in World War II. The Comanche company code talkers also had the Japanese fooled when they talked on "walkie-talkies" in their own Comanche tongue.

Their bravery in fighting and giving their lives helped defeat the enemy. More Indians fought in W.W.II., than any other ethnic group.

A good example was Ira Hayes, the American Indian from the Pima tribe, was one of six Marines, who raised the American flag over the island of Iwo Jima, Japan in 1945 after winning the battle of Iwo Jima, during WWII.

White Buffalo Often Applied to Legend
(Courtesy Dreamstime.com)

CHAPTER TEN
THE CROW INDIAN WAR

The Crow tribe was one of the few Plains Indians to remain neutral and friendly to the Euro-American settlers and U.S. Army for over 50 years and never warred against the United States until 1887. After years of peace with the United States and excellent service as scouts, a brief incursion was staged after a Blackfeet war party of young braves raided the Crow reservation and stole ponies.

A Crow war chief, called Sword Bearer had a vision of protection if he wore his sword.   He led a war party against the Blackfeet to take back their horses, killing many of them.

In triumph, Sword Bearer led his war party to the home of Agent Henry E. Williamson to inform him of their victory. They rode around the agent's home, emitting war-whoops and firing rifles in the air and scaring the occupants; they riddled the house with bullets.

The Agent was angered and came out to make arrests. Sword Bearer fired his rifle in the dirt at his feet. The agent returned home and wired Fort Custer of the attack. It was the start of the Crow War.

The Chief heard that the army was looking to arrest him. Sword Bearer and nearly 20 warriors left the reservation for Fort Custer.

When the soldiers at Fort Custer saw the approaching Crow warriors, they attempted to fire their cannons at them, expecting an attack, but the rain-soaked cannons could not fire.

Sword Bearer believed that his sword could protect him from harm and fled leading his war party into the Bighorn Mountains for the Bighorn River, where it was believed that they had recruited more

Crow warriors. Plenty Coups was apprised of their actions and ordered the Crow police to search for them.

Brigadier General Thomas H. Ruger took command of Forts Custer and McKinney, Wyoming to launch forces into the Bighorns to occupy the Cheyenne reservation to isolate them from the Crow.

General Ruger's men rode into the mountains in search of the hostiles with two Hotchkiss cannons November 4, 1887. The U.S. Army discovered the Crow camp, 3,000 strong. Some of the Crow Scouts had returned to fight with a few hundred soldiers.

Around 10:30 a.m, Ruger gave the Crow time to surrender. Morris directed the peaceable Crow to move up toward the birch tree; the rest were considered hostiles.

All but about 600 warriors moved up. It was a stand-off. Ruger and Dudley, and the 7th Cavalry positioned to fight. Sword Bearer and 150 warriors rode out in a charge against them.

The Crow retreated to a wooded area along the river. The cavalry countered with an attack. The Crow fired on them from 200 yards.

The cavalry exchanged fire with them using Hotchkiss cannons, dumping two inch rounds into their camp. Sword Bearer rode back and forth in front of his warriors and encouraged them to stay. He was hit and wounded by rifle fire.

Some Crows came in and gave up; others remained in the Bighorn Mountains and evaded the soldiers. The hostiles surrendered to the Crow Indian Police, who marched into the Bighorns after them. Sword Bearer's death ended the last and only Crow Indian War with the United States.

148

CHAPTER ELEVEN
CROW MYTHOLOGY

Plains Indian mythology depicts the Crow as the trickster and a crafty bird, who helps Coyote by relaying messages between him and the Creator. The crow was a big part of Crow Indian culture. These are some folk tales told over and over by the Indian storytellers. Old Man Coyote is the Crow Indian's name for their creator hero, Coyote, like the Crow was a trickster in their stories

At the beginning of the world, there was nothing but water. It was dark in the world, and no one saw the water. Then the Old Man of the Crow People came into the world, and he looked all around and said, "Is there nothing in this world but water?

Off in the distance, Old Man saw that there were two little ducks swimming all about. These ducks had red eyes. Old Man called them to them. They swam, paddling in the world of water.

Old Man said to them, "Is there nothing here but water?"
The elder duck answered, "We have never seen anything in this world but water, but we think that there may be something down under the water. We feel it in our hearts."

Dive down, Younger Duck," said Old Man, and he dove under the water, looking for the bottom. He was gone a long time, and Old Man said, "I am afraid that Younger Duck drowned."

"No, said the Elder Duck, "we are able to hold our breath for a long time. He will come back up."

At about that time, Younger Duck came up with something in his bill. It was a root.

"If there is a root, said the Old Man, "then there must be earth as well. Dive down Elder Duck, see if you find some earth."

The elder duck dove deep, and was gone for a long time. When he came up, he had a ball of mud in his bill.

"This is what I have been looking for," said Old Man. He took the root and put it in the ball of wet earth and blew three times on it.

Once he blew, twice and he again blew on the ball of earth.

The ball grew and filled the world and pushed the water aside. It grew until there was a great land, plants and animals living in it. The ducks that live in water, on land, and in the sky, brought up the earth, and Old Man made the world for the Crow Indians.

ᐱ<>ᐱ

Star Boy was a hero of the Crow Indians and other Plains tribes. Grandmother adopted the boy. He was a monster slayer. At the height of his adventures he died. A serpent entered his body until he was a pile of bones and kept him from coming back to life, so Star Boy became the Morning Star.

~<>~

The head chief of a Crow Indian band on the Bighorn River had a gorgeous Indian princess for a daughter, desired by many braves. The chief set a price for her of 100 horses captured in war for bride price.

A young chief truly loved her and tried in vain to bring down the bride price. The princess said that she would die rather than marry another.

Her teepee was next to her parents' lodge and they kept hearing strange noises. When she was asked, the daughter denied anything unusual. In time, the girl became pregnant and could not conceal it from her mother. Finally, the girl admitted to her mother that she was with child. Her father called the council together to handle the family disgrace. They summoned the girl before them. They were amazed that she stood before them unashamed.

She told them how several moons ago a strange that a strange thing had happened to her that had never happened before. She told how she had awakened from her sleep to the sound of hoof beats and scratching in her hearth and blowing the coals into flames.

Then she saw it. It was not human, but a white buffalo. He walked upright on his hind legs to her bed and sat down. The young princess fainted and when she awoke, he had disappeared in the darkness. The girl looked at her father and then the council and continued. He came back from time to time during the full moon, but never hurt her with his hooves or horns. She said that she was too frightened to call out. The girl could not explain her condition to them and could blame no one, but the white buffalo.

Most of the council did not believe her story and none of them had ever seen a white buffalo and could not understand how she got pregnant. Then, a wise old man from the village spoke up.

He told how he had gone to Washington to see the Great Father and saw a great medicine man, who told about a maiden who had gotten pregnant without a man many, many moons ago. Her child was allowed to live and became the greatest medicine man of all time, before they put him to death.

The council did not believe her story and condemned the girl to death, but the young chief convinced them to wait until the next full moon. Then they would know if she spoke the truth. The council named the young chief as the guard of her teepee.

The third night of the full moon, the girl screamed and the young chief ran into her teepee. He saw the white buffalo standing upright with his hoof raised to strike him, but the young chief swung his knife and severed his hoof. The bison struck the young chief with his other hoof, rendering him unconscious. When he awakened, the white buffalo had disappeared.

151

During the night, the old chief had awakened with a start at the sound of a commotion, but still did not believe their story. They saw blood on the ground, but no white buffalo. The next morning, the council concluded to have the girl and the young chief put to death by the hands of the bowmen, the next day.

Their bravest warrior stayed in his lodge all day long and claimed to be ill. He kept his hands under his robes and complained of pain. Early the next day, the maiden entered the ailing warrior's lodge as he slept his arms in sight and saw that his hand was missing.

She quickly ran to the place of the intended execution, where they were preparing to end the young chief's life. He was speaking his last words to the crowd.

The princess shouted stop to the head medicine man. He told them to hold their arrows. The girl told them what she had seen. He told them not to loose his bindings, but would look into it.

They went to the sick warrior's lodge and discovered the severed hoof and pried it open to see the hand inside. The people demanded he be killed. He was taken to the field and shot.

The princess and young chief were exonerated. The chief gave the maiden to the young chief for marriage. Her first child died in breech birth, but they had many healthy children and lived a happy life. The story of the white buffalo remains a mystery.

ᴍ<>ᴍ

A saga of courtship told of a Crow princess named Buffalo Bird Woman and a brave named Red Wing. When she was fourteen years of age, the young Hidatsa woman walked through the village and noticed Red Eagle Wing, a handsome brave. She heard him singing as he swept his lodge; she was sure that he liked her.

One day, the women went to pick berries. His mother told Buffalo Woman's mother that he wished to join them and guard them from their enemies. As they picked berries, the young warrior did not speak to her, but she still expected him to approach her father and offer horses as her bride price for marriage.

152

Many moons passed and they were husking corn. Buffalo Bird Woman sat beside Red Eagle Wing. She wore her best dress and elk tooth necklace. Buffalo Bird Woman thought it would not be bad to have a husband. Red Hand carried her corn bundle back to the village for her; an act that braves did for girls they admired. Buffalo Bird Woman forgot Red Eagle Wing.

The next day as Buffalo Bird Woman carried water from the river, she walked behind Waving Corn, a pretty girl two years her elder. Red Hand wore grass plumes in his hair, a sign he had ridden with a war party. He walked by her and smiled at Waving Corn, instead.

She ran off and hid her tears. Buffalo Bird Woman was passed over in marriage. The next year, when she was seventeen, an old Indian, Hanging Stone came to her father and offered four horses and three flint-lock guns for her hand in marriage; her father refused, saying she was too young to marry. The next day he returned with the same offer, except two of the horses were valuable buffalo horses.

When the man had left, her father asked his wives what they thought, but they left it up to him. He discussed it with Buffalo Bird Woman and accepted Magpie's offer that he had made earlier, instead. He sent a fine war bonnet, a weasel skin cap, and three horses as gifts from the bride's family.

She shyly placed the cap on his head and sat down next to him. The family provided five kettles of food for the feast. The next day the groom's family placed their gifts out for the family of the bride. Buffalo Bird Woman and Magpie were married and had their very own lodge.

~<>~

She was the most beautiful woman in the whole Crow village and had a husband, Chief Big Rain. Many men in the village desired her. Red Arm went directly to Big Rain's lodge. She asked him what he wanted. "I have come here because I love you," he said. "Don't you realize that I belong to the chief?" "Yes, but he doesn't love you like I do. He does not go to war. I will paint your face and bring you horses. As long as you are Big Rain's he will never paint your face." She said,

153

"Big Rain will kill you." Red Arm left Red Cherry's teepee with her ring on his finger. The following day, he led a raid against the Blackfoot. He returned and sent a message. "We will elope tonight. Where shall I meet you?"

They elected to honeymoon while on a Blackfoot raid. Big Rain was angry when they returned with many horses. Big Rain and his six sisters severely beat Red Arm upon his return. Red Arm fell to the ground, during the beating. Had he resisted, they would have been justified in killing him. By their rule, had they drawn blood on him, he could have killed them. One of Red Arm wives scolded him for taking Big Rain's wife, when he could have more. Red Arm said he wanted the most beautiful woman in his lodge.

Red Arm celebrated with a horse dance before joining the raiding party to count coup on the Blackfeet. Big Cherry joined them. Four days later, they returned with a victory and counted three scalps. Big Rain and his sisters flogged him.

He was greeted in his lodge by his wife and new baby boy, who would be brave like his father. Two nights after his reprimand, Red Arm, Red Cherry and many warriors went to steal Blackfoot horses. When he returned, Red Arm was again beaten. This time some warriors that followed Red Arm confronted Big Rain.

"You have flogged him three times now. You will beat him no more. Red Cherry loves him and does not love you. "We will buy your right to her and give her to Red Arm. As a great chief, you would hate to want a woman who loves a warrior more than you." Big Rain still loved her. He released her for one war horse, 10 guns, 10 chief's coats, scarlet cloth, 10 pairs of new leggings, and 10 pairs of new moccasins.

Now, Red Arm had two brides in his lodge.

ᴹ<>ᴹ

Ghosts were incorporated into the Crow society. The people were highly superstitious and strongly believed in ghosts. They believed that an enemy ghost could cause a malady. When an Indian was ill, the condition was often blamed on the presence of a ghost. The Crow

Indians believed that ghosts could cause insanity. Ghosts were not always malevolent. Some ghosts were believed to bring a blessing in visions.

The Crow believed that the spirits lived in a ghost camp near them and that they hooted like owls and appeared in whirlwinds. The owl represented death to them. The Indians highly avoided the whirlwinds.

Some Crow Indians were believed to be ghost people, who could communicate with ghosts and acted as a medium with the nether world. They received payment to handle a ghost situation.

Ghosts were highly feared by Indians. Wives' tales often included stories about ghosts and many ghost stories were told.

~<>~

The character of Raven was sometimes interchanged with Crow. Crow was crafty, watchful and a scavenger that hung around the camp to steal food. The Crow was usually a noisy bird calling from a tall tree looking down on the world, but he could sail silently through the air as the hunter. A favorite subject of storytellers was the old trickster, the Crow.

ᴧ<>ᴧ

The story of how Raven stole the stars follows. Long before the white man, no one lived in America, but the Indians and wild animals and they lived in utter darkness. The Chief and his band dwelt at the mouth of a northern river and horded all of the light.

The Chief kept the stars hidden a bag and he treasured it along with the sun and moon that he kept in special containers. The Chief was like a miser guarding his riches. He declared himself a wealthy man to his people. The Chief reached into his star bag and ran his fingers over the stars inside.

The great Chief revealed the stars to them. They would come near him in awe, as he lifted the lid on one of his precious containers. The light poured out and bedazzled and blinded them.

The poor Indians in the world outside sat in the dark and cold in the darkness, they groped around feeling for berries and roots to eat. They thought that their wretchedness was from the spirits and the poor souls had no knowledge of the sun, moon and stars.

The great Chief was unaware of misery and observed the hungry and naked people, convinced he was all powerful. The wretches begged for some light, but the Chief gave not one star.

In the North, the Raven was born. He flew from his own land and soared over the borders and saw a gleam of light penetrate the darkness across the sky from the hole in the roof of the Chief's lodge.

The Chief had been showing his people the sun, but he closed the lid and the light disappeared. Raven peered through the roof at the Chief, as he pulled the string and dumped the stars out of the bag onto the floor. The light dazzled and brilliance filled the heap. Light resonated around the room. The light shone everywhere. In the light one could see the Chiefs greedy face.

The Chief held the stars in his brown hands and fingered them, lovingly before placing them back in the bag. His people tried to help him, but the Chief hollered at them to stay back.

The Chief slept by the fire that night, as Raven dropped through the smoke hole onto the floor and saw the star bag hanging from a pole. He ceased it in his beak and escaped through the smoke hole. Before long, the bag began to stink. Raven had grabbed a bag of dried fish; he dropped it from his beak.

A starving family of Indians found the bag in the darkness and devoured the fish. They ate ever bit of it. The story of the fall from heaven passed from tribe to tribe and soon all Indians were staring into the sky, waiting for food.

Again Raven returned to the lodge of the great Chief to steal the light for the poor mortals, but the Chief awakened saw him fly down. He cried out and grabbed for the Raven, but wound up with a mere handful of feathers. The trickster eluded him and flew out through the smoke hole in the roof.

156

The frustrated Chief stood there holding a handful of tail feathers, yet knew not why the Raven had come. The mighty Chief ordered the Raven killed and guarded the sun, moon and stars.

The Raven flew about the earth going here and there and saw the desperate mortals with their hands stretched upward to the sky. He longed to bring them the sun, moon, and the stars.

He had a plan and returned to the village of the Chief. Some boys remembered the Chief's order and pounced on him and beat Raven up, but he flew to the top of a tall pine tree. They searched for him, but the trickster turned himself into a pine needle.

The boys ran through the forest to the forbidden spring, where only the Chief's daughter could drink. In fear they ran away and said nothing of the Big Black Bird for fear of reprisal.

The cunning Raven at the top of the pine tree could sit and watch for the daughter of the Chief. Late that day, she arrived with her companions, who had been picking berries and were weary, thirsty, and fell to the ground, exhausted.

The Chief's daughter knelt to get a drink. At that very moment the pine needle freed itself and plummeted into the water. The princess scooped up the pine needle with the water and swallowed it down and knew nothing of the good spirit, who longed to save mankind. The princess returned home and felt ill. She gave birth to n Indian boy child.

The Chief rejoiced, not knowing that his new grandson was Raven in disguise. The proud grandfather gave a feast in celebration. With mixed emotion, he hung the sun and moon on two willow poles beside his house.

As the drums beat incessantly, the Indians observed the light of the sun for the first time. They crawled on the earth in fear of the light and fell on their faces in terror.

The shaman looked for the sky to drop more food. Expecting more food, the Indians danced and sang about food from the sky. The Chief took down the sun and the moon and placed them in their *respective containers. Without the lights in the sky, the Indians sank into despair.*

The boy grew quickly and did not forget the mortals. Raven asked the old Chief, "What is in that bag grandfather?" The Chief took the boy's face in his hands. "What makes you ask?

"Because the bag shines so, grandfather," the boy said.

The Chief said, "I have stars in the bag." Raven pretended not to understand, so the Chief undid the string.

"Cup your two hands together," said the Chief, as he poured the contents into the boy's hands, filling them with stars. After that, Raven could play with them.

He made different designs of squares and triangles and figures of men and deer with them. He rolled them like marbles, playing with them, but always put them back in the bag.

The Chief watched with sharp eyes. All of this time in the body of the boy, Raven plotted to steal the stars, remembering in his heart the poor mortals in the dark.

As the great Chief's daughter slept, the boy slipped out from under his sleeping robe and sneaked into where the star bag hung. He took down the bag without making a sound.

The boy carried the bag outside and changed into Raven, the trickster. Raven picked up the bag in his beak and flew over the sleeping village.

He flapped his big wings and flew higher and higher in the sky. Raven rose up into the heavens flying higher then he dropped the stars across the heavens. The sky immediately was illuminated with a brilliance of dazzling light.

Thousands of stars shone brightly in the sky millions of glittering stars lit up the heavens. The Indians ran into the woods and hid. Some ran into the desert. Others dove into the sea. They had never seen the stars. For some time, they were afraid fearing the lights, but the stars did not fall on them. If one fell, it shot across the sky in a stream.

The shaman explained to the people that the spirits had riddled the sky with holes and soon food would fall down to reach them. They stared up into the heavens for many moons waiting for the food and they received comfort watching the sky and heavens. Patterns in the sky were their invention.

In the meantime, Raven flew back to the village of the Chief and turned back into the boy. He crawled back into his sleeping robes. The boy pretended to sleep. Suddenly, he screamed. His mother jumped up and ran to him, "What is it my son?" she asked, the Chief followed. She held the boy as he cried uncontrollably.

"You were dreaming my son. Your grandfather and I were sleeping until we heard your outcry," his mother said.

The Raven blurted out his story, sobbing. "I was asleep, when I was awakened by a noise like the rushing wind and thunder," he related. Suddenly the whole lodge opened up.

"The lodge still stands young son," said grandfather.

"A huge black bird, whose wings filled the sky, came inside." "You must have had a nightmare," said grandfather.

"He snatched the bag of stars with his beak and flew out. I could not stop him. I screamed," sobbed the boy. The boy began to cry, incessantly. "The stars are gone," he wailed. Grandfather said, "I will show you the stars. It was all a bad dream."

The Chief walked over to where the stars had hung. He gave an outcry. The stars were truly gone. The Chief searched frantically, to no avail. The mother watched as the boy sobbed.

The Chief went into the streets and demanded everyone search for the stars, but they couldn't be found. Then everyone began to look up. The heavens were filled with stars!

∧∧◇∧∧

THE MONTANA CROW INDIAN RESERVATION

The Crow Indians dwelled in southwestern Montana and northern Wyoming in the 1800's and moved onto the Crow Reservation, established on May 7, 1868 by treaty, where it remains, today and lies in Big Horn and Yellowstone counties in south-central Montana.

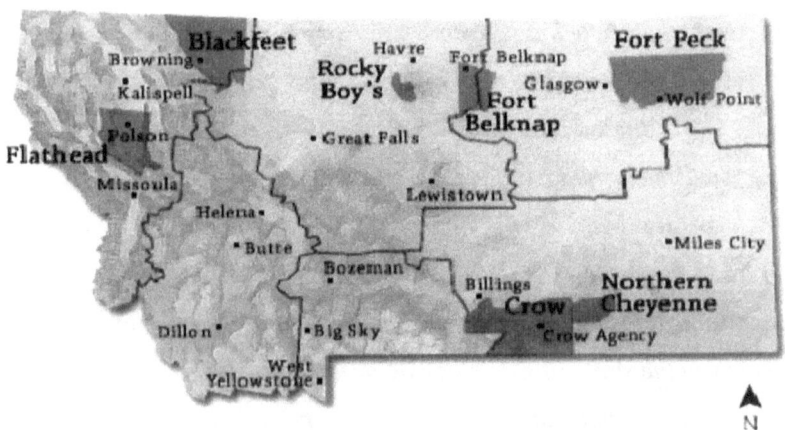

Crow Nation Indian Reservation in Southern Montana
(Courtesy of Visitmt.com)

CHAPTER TWELVE
THE CROW TODAY

The Crow Nation agreed to cede more land to the United States and agreed to move to their present reservation in Montana. The western half of the Crow reservation in southern Montana had been ceded and the Crow Agency had moved there for the third and last time to its present location sixty miles east of Billings, Montana.

The U.S. government had passed the Assimilation Act and the Crow Indians were expected to assume the white man's way of life. The government intended to destroy the Indian and save the man or destroy the culture and save the Indian. Crow adults had to take up farming; this period in Indian history was the "assimilation phase."

Children were taken from their parents to live in white man's boarding schools, educated and were placed in a new environment to live like white children and become Americanized. Schools were run by benevolent societies, churches and the government. Physical separation from their parents was a short distance or thousands of miles to get the Indian children to forget their heritage.

In 1885 Chief Plenty Coups made a trip to Washington D.C. with the demands for his people and again in 1900.

Some of the parents refused to part with their children and kept them with them. Then, two Catholic schools were established on the Crow reserve. In 1887, St. Xavier School was founded and in 1891 St. Charles Mission was built in Pryor, Montana and education was accomplished without their leaving home with numerous Christianity converts among the Indians.

To keep the Indians from being exploited, the government acted as a trustee and ensured that the Indians could not sell their land for 25 years, but they could lease it. The acceptance of government policies meant American citizenship for the Crow Indians.

The socio-political structure of the Crow tribe was a traditional form of government, having a principal chief with additional bands. Prominent leaders were recognized by the order of importance and their lodges were arranged in that order. The United States opposed them practicing their own form of tribal government.

Despite government efforts to help the Indians preserve their lands from 1880-1900, they lost or sold nearly half of their land, which reduced it from 155 million acres down to 78 million acres.

The U.S. government encouraged the Crow chiefs and sub-chiefs to dwell in square houses, so the Indian Agents had houses built for them like the palefaces. Then, they encouraged the Indians to lodge together in square houses in the form of a town as civilized. The Indians preferred the old way. They sat in backrests on dirt floors and used rolled up sleeping mats placed next along the log house walls.

The government gave the Crow 35,531,147 acres for their reservation. They dwelled on the reserve ten years, when the size was reduced to 8,000,400 acres in 1882. Houses were built for them.

The Dawes Act of 1887 altered the relationship of the U.S. government with Indian reservations shaping federal policy to a great degree until the 1930's. The act closed communal reservation land to the Indians and allotted farm tools and 160 acres of their former reservation land was sold to American farmers, miners, and ranchers.

In 1890, the government reduced its size, and paid them $940.000. The last reduction came in 1905, reduced from 2.5 million acres of land to 2,000,000 acres.

The Crow Nation had been asked to give up their lands, so the government could open them up for homesteading and mining. The Crow tribe felt all along that the government had shorted them in the amount of payment. In 1904, they initiated a bill against the U.S. government for just payment for its lands sold. The Court of Indian Claims awarded the Crows $10, 242, 984.70 in compensation.

In 1910-1917, three U.S. Senators sponsored bills to open the balance of the Crow reservation for public settlement in Congress. In every case, their attempts failed. On June 4, 1920, Congress passed an act to divide the reserve into allotments to every tribal member. Crude mountain lands were withheld and retained by the tribe.

Titles for these lands are held in trust by the federal government and the allottees cannot sell their property without approval by the government. The Crow populations now occupy their reservation in south-central Montana. The Crow Indians like other

In the past, the tribe was ruled by a council of chiefs chosen by clan leaders by the council vote for their war honors. Tribal officers were chosen by the vote of the people.

Today, the reservation Crow has a democratic government and a council, laws, Indian police and services. Modern tribal police deal with Indian customs not covered by state and federal laws.

The Crow Indians currently reside near Billings, Montana on their reservation. Most Crow, today speak English, yet the Siouan tongue has not been forgotten and is spoken in their ceremonies.

Today 70% of the Crow Indians speak the Crow language. They maintain the old traditions.

Chief Plenty Coups had become a very successful farmer and rancher; he urged the members of his tribe to join the armed forces and fight during World War I. The Chief had no offspring in his marriage, so he deeded his home to the State of Montana.

In 1928, Chief Plenty Coups visited George Washington's plantation in Virginia and was inspired to donate 195 acres of his land to Big Horn County, near Pryor, Montana. He died in 1932 and is buried in Pryor. His log cabin home and grave site are on the property, now including a museum and visitor's center in the Chief Plenty Coups State Park in Montana.

In 1930, there were approximately 1674 Crows. By 1937, they had grown to 2,173. The rights to the Yellowtail Dam were lost to the Crow tribe in 1950. During the 30's, the Crow benefited from the New Deal government programs. They provided irrigation system for farming. Forests on reservations were improved. Conservation projects for land management were put into effect.

The Crow Nation did not accept the 1934 Reorganization Act and adopted its own constitution in 1948 with a general council form of government. Every two years the council elects four new officers.

After World War II, the Yellowtail Dam was built on the Bighorn and Little Bighorn Rivers by the Bureau of Reclamation. The Crow Tribe has revenue from agricultural land leases, federal programs: gas and oil leases, and mining revenue from the cede strip northeast of the reserve. Natural resources from agricultural lands coal. Forest resources, wildlife and fisheries make additional revenue.

Chief Plenty Coups
(Photograph Courtesy of Nez Perce.com)

Some of the allottees sold to non-Indian parties and helped reduce the size of the reserve to 1,567,189 acres, but since 1962, the reservation bought all lands sold by them. Crow Indian men age 21 and women, age 18 are automatically made tribal members.

The clans are still active, today, ten clans still remain. Naming ceremonies still exist. Clan uncles help make important decisions for their nieces and nephews. The family unit remains strong and the basis for the Crow society. Mothers still head the family, coming from matrilineal.

In 1982 the Crow Nation won the Inherent Sovereignty Case in the Supreme Court. In 1990, the Crow Council voted to give the tribal chairman authority to conduct Crow business in between quarterly meetings and to issue executive orders to hire and fire department heads and program directors and to open and close bank accounts and authorize signatures on checks. Their form of government is a true democracy.

The Crow Tribe has revenue from agricultural land leases, federal programs, gas and oil leases, and mining revenue from the cede strip northeast of the reserve. Natural resources from land, coal, forest resources, wildlife and fisheries make revenue.

In the 1990's, Chief Plenty Coup's log cabin was renovated, the linoleum and wallboard replaced. The exterior of the house was further renovated, repainted, reroofed and rechinked. Electrical fixtures added by ranchers in the 1940's have been removed and the cabin is being restored to appear like original photos the museum retains from that time period. In 1998, the site of his homestead near Billings, Montana was designated as a national historic landmark.

Chief Plenty Coups on His Favorite Horse
(Courtesy of NezPerce.com)

In 1994, the Crow and the Department of the Interior reached an agreement over the 107th Meridian dispute. Back in 1881, government surveyors had made a serious error in the eastern boundary of the Crow reservation.

The Crow has had their land returned to them through an exchange between the state of Montana and the Bureau of Land Management. Approximately 36,000 acres were deleted that should have been included in the reservation. For the discrepancy, the Bureau of Land Management restored the 36,000 acres and established an $85 million trust fund for economic development.

The Annual Crow Fair was established in 1903. On the third week in August annually, the Apersokee tribe holds the Annual Crow Fair, called the "Teepee Capitol of the World," where Natives come from all over the Country. People camp out in teepees and beneath lodge brush-arbors. Romance is in the air for the young.

The Crow Fair continued into the Day of Honor of Chief Plenty Coups, the greatest chief of the Crow Nation held by the friends of Plenty Coups Association around Labor Day. There is music, dancing, great feasting and buffalo meat is eaten.

Stories of Plenty Coups are told by the honored elders and writers of tribal history. The Crow Indians adhere to their old traditions with dancing and drum groups. The Indians dance in their native costumes, hold powwows, and rodeos. Stories are told by story tellers. There is prayer, song, and laughter. The Indians gamble and have entertainment. Games are played and people visit with each other and talk about old times. The Crow Fair is a great time for celebration and festivities.

Chiefs Assemble for Crow Fair
(Photograph Courtesy of Azusa Publishing, LLC)

White-Man-Runs-Him retired to the Crow Indian reservation near Lodge Grass, Montana, where he lived out his life. He was Joe Medicine Crow's stepfather and the grandfather of Pauline Small, the first woman to be a member of the Crow Nation Council. She carried the flag of the Crow Nation during the Crow Fair Parade.

Today, there are four Catholic churches, two Baptist missions and two Mormon stakes on the reservation. Recently Full Gospel, Pentecostal and other evangelical churches on the reservation.

The Crow in the Lodge Grass Montana area are called, "the people in the valley of the chieftains." Many chiefs came from there, Medicine Crow, Old Dog, Spotted Horse, and Wolf Lays Down.

In February of 1995, there were 9,155 members of the Crow Nation. About 72% live on the reservation in southern Montana primarily in the Bighorn and Little Bighorn River valleys.

Before 1953 membership included 1/64 Crow blood members. Those born after 1953 are expected to be ¼ Crow blood to become members.

The Crow reservation in Montana has 2,235,092 acres. The Tribal tribe owns 445,699 acres, allotment recipients own 1,660,590 acres and non-Indians own 34% of the reservation.

Plenty Coups said, "Education is your most powerful weapon. With education you are the white man's equal; without education you are his victim."

Some Indian reservations are a place of poverty and despair. Education has been a tool to turn that around. It remains to be the key to the future and success on the reservation. All education came in the form of private and public education. Crow high schools are in

Hardin, Lodge Grass, and Pryor, Montana. Lodge Grass and Pryor have Indian school boards.

Little Bighorn College at the Crow Agency has been successful since the mid 1970's. The college is now a four year school. Over 400 Crow students have graduated there.

The Bureau of Reclamation has set up a trust fund with revenues from the Yellowtail Dam providing $100, 000.00 a year for higher education scholarships for tribal members of the Crow Nation.

Enrolled tribal members receive a mandate per-capita payment three times a year. The payments cause a drain on tribal revenues and capitol that would have been used in Crow projects. The per-capita payment reduces revenue, which would be used for various substantial land purchase programs on the Crow reservation.

A number of service businesses in the small communities of Crow Agency, Lodge Grass, and Pryor, the tribal government, Little Bighorn College and gaming provide jobs.

The U.S. Congress passed the Indian Gaming Regulatory Act (IGRA), which provided for the operation of businesses for gaming by tribal governments in 1998.

It also established an independent federal regulatory authority for gaming on Indian lands. Casinos have been opened and are providing many new jobs for the unemployed Crow Indians. The tribe has adapted over time to adversity and change and show considerable promise for a good future ahead.

The Crow tribe today is self governed. There are Casinos that hire a lot of Crow people. They farm and own businesses and College is available for the young people to get a good education.

GLOSSARY

ABRADER-a fine stone used as a delicate abrading stone to polish.

AMULET- was a charm worn around the neck to ward off evil.

ARROWHEAD-an arrow point chipped from chert or obsidian.

ATLATL-an ancient wooden throwing device used too thrust a spear.

AWL-pointed tools, made from bone, stone or wood for sewing.

AXE-an adze made of stone, hafted in a handle used to chop wood.

BOLA- stones tied to a cord, thrown to ensnare an animal's legs.

BOILING STONE-fiery-hot stones put into a water vessel for cooking.

CRESCENT-crescent shaped arrowhead used to hunt geese on water.

DRILL- stone drill head used with bow-drill for drilling bone or stone.

DRILL CUP-hand-held cupped stone to hold bow-drill shaft to drill.

FETTISH-sacred carved stone animal used for luck in hunting.

FLESHING KNIFE-combined hide scraper & knife used for fleshing.

GAME STONE-stone game piece used to play games or gamble.

GRAVER-sharp stone used to incise bone, wood or stone.

HAND AXE-celt shaped to fit the hand used for cutting.

HIDESCRAPER-a flat stone flaked on the edge used to flesh hides.

HOE-a flat triangular stone affixed to a handle used to make furrows.

MANO-a small flat stone used with a mortar to grind food.

REAMER-a bone drill used in enlarging holes in bone, shell, and stone.

SHAFT SMOOTHER-a polished groove stone used to smooth arrows.

SPEARHEAD-a large stone projectile point used on a spear.

STONE KNIFE-a stone-age flint knife used in hunting and war.

STONE SHOVEL-a crude shovel chipped from chert used for digging.

MORTAR-a large stone used with a pestle for grinding.

NEEDLE-a sharp piece of bone with an eyelet used to sew clothing.

NET WEIGHT-a drilled or grooved stone used as a fishing net weight.

POUNDER- a heavy stone used as a maul or to pound.

QUIRT-a leather whip used as riding gear with horses.

TOMAHAWK- a war axe of stone, hafted in a handle for a war club.

INDEX

BIBLIOGRAPHY

Andrews, Elaine, *The First Americans, Indians of the Plains*, Benford Books, Inc., New York, 1992.

Ayre, Robert, *Sketco the Raven*, Scholastic-Tab Publications, LTD, Richmond Hill. Ontario, 1974.

Bryan Jr., William L., *Montana Indians, Yesterday and Today*, 2*nd* Edition, American & World Publishing, Helena, 1996.

Capps, Benjamin, *The Great Chiefs*, Time-Life Books, Alexandria, Va., 1980.

Convis, Charles L., *Native American Women*, Pioneer Press, Carson City, 1996.

Convis, Charles L., *Warriors & Chiefs of the Old West*, Pioneer Press, Carson City, 1996.

Barnes, Dr. Ian, *The Historical Atlas of Native Am*ericans, Chartwell Books, Inc., New York, 2010.

Fitzgerald, Michael and Judith, *Indian Spirit*, World Wisdom Inc. Bloomington, Indiana, 2006.

Graham, Col. W.A., *The Story of the Little Bighorn*, Bonanza Books, New York, 1959.

Grant, Bruce, *Concise Encyclopedia of the American Indians*, Random House, New York, 1958.

Haines, Francis, *The Buffalo*, Thomas Y. Crowell Company, New York, 1834.

Linderman, Frank B., *Plenty Coups, Chief of the Crows*, Bison Books, New York, 1932.

Lowie, Robert H., *The Crow Indians*, University of Nebraska Press, Lincoln, 1983.

Lowie, Robert H., *Indians of the Plains*, Mcgraw Hill Book Company, New York, 1954.

Medicine, Crow, Joseph & Herman J. Viola, *The Crow Indians Own Stories, From the Heart of the Crow Country*, Orion Books, New York, 1992.

Taylor, Colin F., *The Plains Indians*, Crescent Books, New York, 1994.

Thorp, Raymond W. and Bunker, Robert, *Crow Killer, The Saga of Liver-Eating Johnson*, University of Indiana Press, Bloomington, 1983.

Wert, Jeffry D., *The Controversial Life of George Armstrong Custer*, Simon & Schuster, New York, 1996.

CITING ELECTRONIC PUBLICATIONS

<http://access geneology.com/native/tribe/crow/crowhist.com>
<http://access geneology.com/native/tribes/crow/crowhist.htm>
<http://anthro.palomar.edu/kinship_6.htm>
<http://astonisher.com/archives/museum/hairy_moccasin_big_horn.html>
<http://bigorrin.org/crow_kids.htm>
<http://desertusa.com/mag99/may/papr/crook.html>
<http://electriccityweblog.com/?p=2937>
<http://enwikipedia.org/wiki/Plenty_Coups>
<http://fortlincoln.org/fort_ab_history.aspx>
<http://fortmacleod.com/visiting/history/default.cfm>
<http://fourdir.com/crow.htm>
<http://hmdb.org/marker.asp?marker=33923>
<http://legendsofamerica.com/mt-forts.html>
<http://lewisandclarktrail.com/section2/ndcities/willistonfunion.htm>
<http://lib.ibhc.edu/about/history/timeline.php>
<http://lib.ibhc.edu/about/history/crowchiefs.php>
<http://lib.ibhc.edu/about/history/4.00.php>
<http://nps.gov/bica/istoryculture/the-crow-nation.htm>
<http://indians.org/articles/crow-indians.html>
<http://nrcprograms.org/site/PageServer?pagename=airc_res_mt_crow>
<http://onewest.net/~tillman/shoshone/butte.htm>
<http://pbs.org/weta/thewest/people/a_c/crook.htm>
<http://plentycoups.org/educate/content//msocstudies.html>
<http://prattrolf.blogspot.com/2009/04crow-creation-story>
<http://us7thcavof.com/Scouts.html>
<http://snowwowl.com/nativeleaders/plentycoups.html>
<http://snowwowl.com/peoplecomanche.html>
<http://us7thcavcof.com/scouts.html>
<http://wollfcountry.net/information/WolfPack.html>

Author explores inside of a 19th century
stone house in southeastern Oregon.
About the Author

Born in Lexington, Nebraska, Robert Bolen, B.A. has a degree in Archeology/Anthropology. In an Archeology class, he was informed that because of his features, the Mongolian eye-fold, he was part Indian. In 1755, a Bolen ancestor was taken captive by Delaware Indians. She was later rescued with her baby daughter, Robb's Great, Great, Grandmother. At the time of rescue, the poor girl (just 17) was scalped, but she lived. The French scalp was the size of a silver dollar. Family says that she combed her hair hiding the scar and managed to live to be well over one hundred. Bolens served under George Washington in the American Revolution. In 1777, the author's ancestors erected Fort Bolin, near Cross Creek, Pennsylvania for protection from Indian attacks. Two ancestors were killed in Kentucky by Shawnee Indians allied to the British. Great Gran-dad Gilbert Bolen rode with the Ohio Fourth Cavalry in the Civil War under General Sherman. In 1866, Gilbert brought his wife and six children west to Nebraska in a Conestoga wagon. Gran-dad Denver Colorado Bolen knew Buffalo Bill Cody in western Nebraska. Bolen is an authority on Indian artifacts and glass trade beads. Robb and Dori Bolen reside in Nampa, Idaho, near Boise. Robb owns the website, Fort Boise Bead Trader.com.

PHOTOGRAPHS
COURTESY OF
AZUSA Publishing, LLC
3575 S. Fox Street
Englewood, CO 80110

Email: azusa@azusapublishing.com

Phone Toll-free: 888-783-0077

Phone/Fax: 303-783-0073

Email: azusa@azusapublishing.com

Mailing address: P.O. Box 2526, Englewood, CO 80150